# Freya

## LADY WOLF

### GREEN MAGIC

Green Magic
53 Brooks Road
Street
Somerset
BA16 0PP
England
www.greenmagicpublishing.com


Designed and typeset by Carrigboy, Wells, UK
www.carrigboy.co.uk


ISBN 978-1-915580-39-9

# GREEN MAGIC

## THIS BOOK IS DEDICATED TO:

BRIAN MAX

My King, Person, Best Friend, My Rock,
Soul Mate, Twin Flame, Husband and My Always and
Forever – You have shown me what true love is!

Thank you for allowing me safe space to explore and step
fully into my liberation.

Thank you for dancing beside me and howling with me in
celebration!

Thank you for seeing me in all my raw, gloriously fucked up
authenticity, and for loving me!

Thank you for the laughter, bonfires and real talks.

Thank you for crossing many oceans to find me in the desert.

# Introduction

Every book becomes a memoir! An exploration. An embodiment! When I write, it becomes a ritual. A channelling. A meditation through activation. After my thirteen-month experience of intentionally channelling chaos while I was actively birthing my *Loki – Chaos or Catalyst?* book, I thought I was prepared for all that life would thrust upon me. At least, I thought I should have been a bit more prepared.

Moving with Loki intentionally for thirteen months was intense! Embracing the essence of chaos as one would a lover was explosive! When my Loki book was complete, I had a sense of calm but also a lingering sense that something big was about to surface.

Freya came to me in the midst of my divorce. Yes, thank you Loki for being the catalyst in ending my 24-year toxic marriage and helping me to see the hard truths, the necessary reality, and for propelling me with a bit of resistance to really embrace the chaos of closing one door and moving forwards towards the unknown future as a liberated woman.

This book is my liberation activation! It is my ode to those single souls out there who think they can't find love after heartache. This book highlights my journey with Freya as she awakened the sexual prowess and Sovereign Queen within me, which allowed me to experience bliss, taste passion and find the kind of love that most people have stopped believing in.

It is my intent that you find within these pages an anchor of inspiration, lessons from myths, mirrors, tips and techniques to really see your own inner Freya and to move forward in your day-to-day lives with a bit more confidence and stamina, and to become a lover of your one wild, untamed life.

LADY WOLF

# Table of Contents

CHAPTER ONE

# Freya

ᚠ

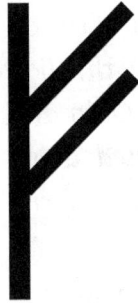

Freya – the name itself translates as 'lady'. Most know of Freya from Norse Mythology as the Goddess of Sex, Lust, Passion, Love, Beauty, War, Death, Magic, Wealth, Independence, Eroticism, Clairvoyance and Sensuality. As with all deities, she is multifaceted, and where she stems from in mythology there really is no concrete proof that she or any of the 'old gods/goddesses' actually existed on the mortal plane.

For the sake of this book, we will be exploring Freya as just that – a figure, character and concept from ancient myths. As humans and modern practitioners of Wicca, Heathenism and those who study Norse Paganism, we are constantly outsourcing and searching for something greater than ourselves to believe in – *"myths give us a voice when our own inspiration fails."* Freya's multifaceted attributes described in these stories and myths that are man-written will become our inspiration for transposing them as a mirror, giving us a voice to activate those attributes within our individual selves and lives.

## HER 'STORY'

*"Freya is the daughter of the Sea God Njord and the sister of Frey. In one such myth, Njord calls to his twin children to introduce them to Odin and the other Aesir (old term for gods). They floated down with a fluttering, arms linked, as their father referred to them as 'Summer & Beauty'.*

*Frey was made to be king and master of the schooling of the Light Elves, spending most of his time in Alfheim, the Realm of Elves. Freya stayed in the city of Asgard. She was well-known and adored for her elaborate palace, where she would entertain guests that came to admire her beauty, music and charisma."*

From this short introduction, it appears that Freya was meant to just be seen as something beautiful and someone to be admired as a gracious and entertaining hostess. When we take the time to dive in a bit deeper into myths and stories, we can begin to know Freya as someone with more depth.

In order to do this, though, we need to broaden our own minds and rely less on the words from the past as factual and begin to formulate a more modern perspective on how to transmute these somewhat ancient writings into something applicable to today's world.

"These stories, often populated by gods, heroes, monsters, and mystical creatures, reveal the psyche of ancient civilizations and provide insight into how these societies viewed themselves, their world, and the forces that shaped their existence.

Through an exploration of several key myths and legends from different cultures, we can uncover how these narratives served as mirrors reflecting the cultural, moral, and spiritual landscapes of their times."

Joshua Napilay (medium.com)

The challenge in transmuting myths and stories from the past to the present comes when we cannot disengage from gatekeeping. In my personal experience as a modern-day practitioner of Wicca and an active priestess representing three different lineages, I have found more gatekeepers than I have open-minded individuals.

Gatekeeping is defined as "the process of controlling information." In today's society, we see gatekeeping and gaslighting as interchangeable behaviors. In tight-knit religious circles, covens, groves, and specific Wiccan practices, the act of gatekeeping centers more on secrets and deeming who is privileged to certain information.

The term 'toxic witches' is rapidly spreading as more and more practitioners move into the center stage of social media platforms. These supposed toxic witches seem to hold an authority and knowledge that gives them supremacy over others. With this (often self-proclaimed) power, they can then decide another person's worth and demand obedience and compliance.

In the past two decades that I have been practicing, I have seen more of these practitioners than I have not. Being told in any kind of religious practice what one can believe, how one can practice, and who one can associate with outside of these practices is control – a level of control that most of us that seek the pathways of Paganism, Heathenism, and anything outside of the structured and organized religions resist!

Witchcraft is the fastest-growing practice in the world today. We can naturally speculate that individuals are no longer interested in being told what they should believe or how they are to dress, eat, and live amongst society, based on these beliefs, stipulations, and dogmas being preached.

Organized religions are boxes! These boxes, while they may give insight, hope, and a greater belief in something other than one's ego, are limiting. People do not want to be controlled. People no longer want to answer to someone else when it comes to their personal salvation or spiritual progress.

Growing up in the very structured religious state that is Utah, I was bombarded with rules and stipulations, and faced the wrath of a very condemning, jealous, angry God. When I left that church at the age of sixteen, it was with encouragement from my father and with the hunger for liberation and freedom.

Unfortunately, these religious wounds are hard to disconnect from, and as humans we still carry old belief patterns into new practices. What I have witnessed are individuals leaving one organized religion and stepping into another less structured religious practice. Yet, someone is always in charge. There is always a priest or priestess to answer to, and it appears to be a multi-level scheme not so different from the box one was fleeing.

How can we as modern-day practitioners escape this mindset and harmful pattern? With witchcraft being the fastest-growing practice, most individuals are solitary in an attempt to not deal with gatekeeping and gaslighting. For the first decade of my practice, I found solace in solitary work.

In my second decade, I found excitement, fulfillment, and camaraderie in coven work and group settings. However, looking back at the three lineages I was ordained into and utilizing hindsight as my teacher, I can see that each of these constructs/groups was just as limiting and controlling as the organized box I had desired to escape from.

Here I am in the beginning of my third decade as a self-proclaimed Pagan (or my preferred identification label, 'Animist'), and once again my views have shifted, and, once again, I find myself in a state of mind where I want to flee and escape the limiting boxes.

While writing this book, my life and practice shifted simultaneously. Moving through something tumultuous like a divorce and outsourcing for inspiration and a deity that could highlight within me attributes that I deserved, needed, and was ready to step into was not a challenge. Freya was 'The One!' Her energy was a battle cry screaming within every fiber and cell of my body, not to mention my soul.

Freya is multifaceted, like all deities. As individuals, we too are multifaceted. There is no ONE WAY, ONE GOD – at least, not for me. There is no one way to move through a divorce or one way to explore life after divorce. There simply is no 'one way' of doing or being. In the moment of seeking healing, independence, and ownership of my body, life, and future, Freya stood out.

Freya is one who stands whole and holy within herself. She loves deeply and yet is not bound by her attachment to another. She is queen, confident in her body, and sexually she is a force. Who doesn't want to be royalty within their own castle? Who doesn't want to be confident physically and sexually? Who doesn't want to be a force within this life? Who doesn't want the confidence to love oneself in a world that teaches us to literally despise and reject our very essence, that which makes us unique?

Diana Paxson, a world-renowned expert on Asatru and all things Norse Paganism, and a good friend who stood in my most recent ordination ritual, describes Freya as a "Goddess of Life" and one who will survive Ragnarok and help rebuild the new world.

Freya is guardian of the Vanir, a pantheon of gods responsible for predicting futures, obtaining wealth, increasing fertility, and utilizing wisdom. The Vanir gods are somewhat more poised, unlike the Aesir, who are battle-focused. This grouping of gods consists of:

- Njord – Freya's father and God of the Sea and Winds
- Freyr – Freya's brother, God of Prosperity and Sunshine
- Freya – Goddess of Beauty, Foresight, Sex, and Battle
- Skadi – Goddess of Winter, Mother of Wolves
- Gerdr – Freyr's wife, a Jotun (giantess)
- Odr – Freya's mysterious husband, whose name means 'Divine Madness'

- Hnoss – Goddess of Desire, Freya's daughter with Odr
- Gullveigr – Seidr, Sorceress of Dark Magic

When the Aesir and Vanir fought a great battle over the mistreatment of Gullveigr, a truce was formed. Freya was part of that truce along with her brother. They were *peace treaties* amongst the two groups of gods.

Freya's name means 'lady' and also 'beloved'. She was well-known for opening her great hall to everyone. Her name simply highlights her ability to function at a higher level, where she embodies her ability to honestly love everyone. She is the manifestation of love. Jan Fries writes that "Love is an emotion people produce for themselves." Do we as individuals really produce love for ourselves?

In this world of chaos and constant battles, we as humans moving through the turmoil seem to be seeking love. Marriages end – most often because of a lack of this emotion, whether by one party or by both. My marriage ended ten years prior to the actual filing of paperwork. Love was not an active emotion, nor, looking back, could I say that I indeed felt that emotion. Honestly, I didn't give it that emotion either, not to myself or my relationship.

If Freya was going to be a mirror for me, then I would need to start loving myself.

Filing legal documents was just the beginning of showing myself the love that I had been starved of for two decades. Not just from my ex but from myself. Holding myself accountable for the end and this new beginning was going to require strength, confidence, queenly poise, and determination.

In the two-plus decades of researching and actively working with deities of all pantheons in a way of expanding my knowledge, gaining insight, and seeking that *something* that was larger than my own self and ego, I can honestly say that I never worked with Freya. While I was familiar with her and knew somewhat of her essence, she was not a deity that I felt called to. That is, until the paperwork was filed.

Looking back at this, it makes me sad. Maybe the reason I never felt her call was because I never really embodied a feeling of honest love for myself or my spouse. Our marriage was more like a business arrangement, motivated by the societal norm for a single mother to seek out a father, get married, have more children, and move through the motions of being a 'happy family'.

Was there love? What is love? This question was asked to me just this morning: "Was I in love in my marriage?" My response was no. When we sit back and take inventory of our lives and circumstances, we can really activate hindsight and see a bit more clearly. Oftentimes, it takes a comparison to really see the distinct differences that allow the truths to surface.

Sitting with this question shook me for a bit. Had I been living a lie for two decades? For two decades I was a wife and mother.

Engrossed in being a good, supportive, and devoted wife and engrossed in being a gentle and nurturing mother. These were roles – roles I was living in a manner that society would deem good or bad. But was there love?

My children were my everything. While I can admit that I was not a good mother, nor did I want to simply be just a mother, or a wife, for that matter; as a human, I did the best I could. I loved my children in a way that is indescribable. As a mother, I failed my children in many ways because I was not living my life fully. My existence was focused on being a mother, living a role – a role that was determined by society, upbringing, and anything but my own interpretation of what that role needed to be for me as an individual and for my children.

When we ditch the societal roles and the heavy weight that comes with them, something begins to burst through the cracks of disappointment, pain, and heartache. That bursting is love. My children, now all adults in their twenties, were supportive and happy when I finally divorced, as they had grown up seeing their parents do nothing but fight and be in constant battle. My role of mother was no longer necessary, not on the level it once was.

Throwing away the ownership and title of being someone's wife was liberating and scary! Who was I outside of that role? For two decades, I was wearing a costume and moving through the motions. I was not living! At least, I was not living my life and my truth. There is no time like the present to act in demand of liberation. This was my big moment, my time to reclaim all that I had willingly given up for the sake of others, and truly embody love for myself!

In looking to Freya as a mirror of all that I was now free to be, I was excited, invigorated, and somewhat apprehensive. Ultimately, my determination to live this second half of my life for me propelled me forward and unknowingly into the reality of real love and my greatest adventure.

# CHAPTER TWO

# Rite of Invitation

ᚠ

Deity work is a very personal relationship between the seeker and the deity. While there may be covens, mentors, and books that highlight a 'specific' way to activate connection with a deity, it really is something profoundly unique to the individual and their personal craft. Please honor your authenticity and your solitary practice as you move forward in your crafting of your beliefs and ceremonies.

As a priestess, and one who has been working with deities the past two-plus decades, I have experienced excellent advice, tips, and techniques, and I have utilized many of these within my personal practice. Deity work often begins with asking oneself: "Why, who, and how?"

Why are you the seeker feeling called to reach out beyond your own self to a figure that may or may not exist? Deities, after all, are not proven to be actual people of the flesh. The dictionary defines 'deity' as "a god or goddess" (in polytheistic religions), "divine status, quality, or nature," and "the creator and supreme being."

Defining one's reason as to 'why' outsourcing for a deity as a mirror is the best and most ideal place to begin. For me, seeking Freya was the obvious reflection.

24 years is a very long time to be invested in a companionship and relationship. Walking away from that filled me with a bombardment of emotions and wounds, and hopes for the future required a strong, powerful, confident, wise, sexual liberator as my inspiration.

As I sat there next to my soon-to-be ex, waiting for our virtual courtroom appearance to make our divorce finalized, the one thing on my mind was, "Who am I once I walk out this door?" It was a bit unnerving! How curious that a 24-year marriage filled with so much pain, heartache, happy memories, and terrible moments could be done in a matter of 52 days, a 35-dollar processing fee, and a ten-minute conversation with a judge.

While I stood in the bathroom, moments after the court session ended, I looked into the mirror and asked that question out loud, "Who am I now?" What I felt was a question in return, "Who do you want to be?" While I ate my breakfast with my now ex sitting across from me at the diner, I really gave that some thought.

Key words, attributes, and ideals kept popping into my mind with each bite of my bittersweet breakfast. I wanted to move forwards strong, powerful, confident, wise, sexually liberated, and inspired to claim my independence. I needed a 'cover girl' – someone tangible to see and utilize as my mirror to help me shift these attributes from simply a want to my reality.

As a practitioner of Seidr (a type of divination and sexual magic believed to be practiced by the Norse of the Late Scandinavian Iron Age), Freya was really the only option. In my years as a public figure and high priestess, I have channeled Freya lightly for specific ceremonies in the past, but this would be a different kind of embodiment.

This wasn't going to be 'performative spirituality' – this was going to be personal, and I knew on the surface that calling in Freya was going to create movement within my life on very deep levels. But I arrogantly dismissed the knowing that this movement would not always play out in my favor, on the surface level, that is.

Deity work is nothing new. People have been looking to deities as inspiration, mirrors, and ideals to worship since the beginning of time. However, as humanity has evolved, so too have the deities. Our earliest ancestors looked to the animals as the first gods.

"The worship of animals as godlike beings or deities appearing in animal form is a theriomorphic belief and most commonly known as being practiced by the Egyptians. However, we see this phenomenon present in many religions, such as Hinduism, Buddhism, and even Christianity. It begs one to ask if the early civilizations actually worshiped animals, or did they honor them as a vital tool necessary for their survival?"

Do we as modern-day practitioners still 'worship?' Witchcraft is the fastest-growing practice in the world today. I emphasize the word **'practice'**, as more and more people are turning their backs on organized religion – myself included. Terms like 'worship' are often met with a knee-jerk reaction. This primarily stems from one's childhood and how we were often taught one way to practice, one god to believe in, and only one way to worship and speak to that god.

This modality of 'one size fits all' and 'only one way is the right way' is no longer applicable in our modern world. As a society, we have advanced towards an individual self-realization that we are the only ones capable of shifting things in our lives. This is a powerful progression and much needed, even though we as humans step into our ego selves and slip into old habits.

The term 'worship' is one that needs to be self-defined and nothing more. For some, worship means having reverence and adoration for a deity, while for others, it can mean bowing down to and praying to a deity from a lower status, seeing the deity as one with an elevated status – deity being "an almighty, all-knowing, omnipotent, supreme being."

So your next question in deity work is, "Who?" Who do you as an individual want to work with, see as a mirror, and worship if you choose, as you define that word? All too often, people invest far too much energy into explaining their individual practice to others. One person's solitary craft and spirituality is not open for discussion, nor is it anyone's business. So please take the time to really honor your craft and attach your own meaning to specific words as you move forward, embodying your spirituality into fruition.

Deity work isn't ideal for many. There is a deep Christian wound and profound resistance to gods/goddesses, and that is understandable. Where I live, in Southern Utah, my state is primarily Christian. Most Pagans that are new to the craft have walked away from organized religious constructs and are simply seeking nature as an ally, which is why many turn back to animism as a preferred anchor.

Animism is the belief that "all aspects of nature are divine and sentient." Thus, the animals become the teachers once again. In my first book, *Animals as Gods*, I dove into this practice intensively. Again, you are the only one that can and should define your practice. If you choose to attach labels, then do it for you, and don't waste time explaining it to others.

Myself, I have disconnected from organized religious structures and constructs.

Animism is a title that I have embraced, yet I still do deity work. There is no right or wrong way of doing, there is simply the 'doing', and if it brings you peace, then you are actively living your craft, and that's all that matters.

So, how do you find your "who?" Well, ask yourself just like I did – who in mythology do you look to for inspiration? Who from mythology and history can you embrace as a mirror that is applicable to your current situation?

Most practitioners of the craft have a basic understanding of the different pantheons, myths, and sagas, and there are hundreds of thousands of different gods, goddesses, and animals to choose from. The key is in seeing the attributes they possess as ones you already possess. That's where the mirror work comes into play and the activation will take place. You get to realize that nothing outside of yourself can shift your reality. Everything outside of yourself is simply a reflection of what you already contain.

As one who actively makes lists, I begin deity work with written intention, moving through the question of, "What am I wanting to embody at this current moment in my life?" Writing things down creates a tangible agreement between me and the universe. It becomes a living spell and helps me to stay focused on my intention.

Once I make my list, I like to sit and listen. With this current situation, Freya was already coming through. Her 'essence', her strengths, and her attributes were exactly what I needed, was going to seek, and felt at the time that I was fully ready to embody.

As a ritual priestess, I find moving through an intention ceremony to be the most profound activation experience. With my choice being a call to Freya, I was determined to move through this channeling with all the tools in my arsenal.

So I gathered up some candles, string, paper, pens, and stones, and I prepared the altar, my intention being to engage in a ceremonial cord-cutting.

As beings of energy, we interact with other beings of energy and formulate energetic cords, strings, and/or tethers. Even in our casual encounters, a tiny thread can weave between two people. For me, I was going to cut a 24-year-old tether that was heavy with emotional charges.

To cut a cord and sever an energetic connection, each practitioner has their own style and method, and there is no right or wrong way. Social media likes to offer us the performative version of taking two candles, one to represent each person, tying a string around them and then burning them. Watching as the string literally burns and separates the two candles, this is a way to really visualize the disconnect and separation. However, as with all things, the individual must hold firm to the intention, not just the visual.

There were questions that I needed to really sit with before moving forward with the ceremony. Once I sat with them, I was ready. Calling in Freya as my mirror meant embodying her confidence and strength – both attributes that I currently was not feeling at the moment. But I desperately needed them in order to pull away from this relationship and move into my new life as a single, independent woman.

Performing ceremony skyclad or in the nude can be very vulnerable and very empowering! While I knelt at my altar, completely naked, I began to visualize my intention, and I began with my candles. I selected a red candle to represent me as an individual wounded but ready to embrace my inner solo flame. For my ex, I selected a blue candle to represent a calm healing. I then took some string and tied the two candles together, placing them in the center of my altar.

Using two separate pieces of paper, I wrote down what I was igniting as I ventured forward, away from this union, and on my ex's paper, I wrote down things I was grateful for from our relationship. My paper was placed beneath my candle. With his paper, I did a binding. While I wanted to express gratitude, I did not want to feed any future energetic attachments. So, I began to fold the paper away from me into thirds. Then I bound the folded paper with string and set it aside.

Creating a safe space or a container for ceremonial magick or spellcasting should always be unique to the individual. My circle casting consists of a call to the elemental directions. In a bowl on my altar I had salt, dried mugwort, and a small ceramic container filled with dirt from the center of my yard. It was time to call Freya! It was time to disconnect from my past and move forward! While still on my knees, with both candles lit, I reached my arms above my head.

"I call to Freya, Goddess of Confidence.
Help me to stand whole within myself as a sovereign
single queen.
I call to Freya, Goddess of Knowing.
Help me to see and embrace the closing of one door
and the opening of new ones.
I call to Freya, Goddess of Battle.
Help me to soften my war cries and begin to speak my truths.
I call to Freya, Goddess of Strength.
Help me to move forward, knowing that I will conquer."

As I stood tall, I began to feel a shift within myself. I was ready. I watched as the candles began to burn faster, reaching the string and burning away the connection. I visualized my ex going one way and my path taking me in the opposite direction. In my heart, I honored the pain and gratitude and allowed myself to let go of what was to allow a clean space to be created. Each candle stood unattached!

When I picked up the paper of my ex, I lit it on fire with his flame and wished him well on his journey, out and away from what we once had.

The completion of a ceremony doesn't end right away. While the candles burned down and I tasted the salt on my lips and burned the mugwort to allow a safe and protected disconnect, I knew that the next few days, if not weeks, would be healing and, at the same time, a challenge.

Anytime you move through a cord-cutting, the other person, if they are receptive and aware, will feel it! Typically, they will reach out or start making efforts that they should have made in the relationship to begin with. Both of these happened almost instantly!

My ex came home, as he was living in my guest house in the backyard and both our adult children still lived with us. As I put on my robe and went into the kitchen, he greeted me with a smile and a hello … NOPE! It's all too easy to slip into old habits, especially 24 years of old habits and unhealthy patterns. Placing a hand on my heart, I took in a deep breath and remembered that I was now a sovereign single queen, which meant I was and always have been in control of who I interact with and exchange energy with. So, I took a deep breath, gave him a nod, and went into the other room.

Disengagement, energetically, is like putting up a stop sign and demanding that the other person backs off. This home was NOW my castle, and I would not allow him space within it, and he felt that in that moment and left.

To embody the attributes of any deity, one must do just that! Freya is not a light and fluffy deity – she is a queen!

One who knows her self-worth, one who is confident. In the next few weeks she would challenge me to rise up and really remind myself that I too was a queen. I too knew my self-worth, and I too was going to keep embodying those truths with confidence.

In life, we save ourselves! There is no knight in shining armor that is going to ride in and rescue you. Sorry to burst that bubble! Divorce happens! Not every relationship is meant to last. Learning to walk away with your head held high, confident and with gratitude, is power! This was my big moment! The ceremony was just frosting on a cake that I had been baking for a while! My relationship was done, papers signed. The battles were fought, and this was not a loss. This was in many ways a win for both of us. This was my rite and right of invitation, activation, and initiation.

"Healing is taking your power back and using it to move forward."

Morgan Richard Olivier

Seeing the reality of a situation, holding oneself accountable, and utilizing the lessons instead of anchoring into blame and victimhood is the act of a queen, and I was beyond ready!

# CHAPTER THREE

# Amber Eyes

ᚠ

They say that the eyes are the window to one's soul. About six months post-divorce, a mutual acquaintance of mine and my ex approached me while I was out dancing with my friends and inquired how my ex was doing. After refusing to engage in answering, he responded with, "I don't need to even ask how you are doing – your eyes have never looked so happy." What a compliment!

What is the essence and power of our eyes? Most people have been taught to avoid eye contact, while some are encouraged to really see into another by maintaining intense eye contact. When you really allow yourself to connect with another and you look into each other's eyes, you can see the pupils dilating. In my training as a hypnotherapist, I was taught that this exchange created a bond of trust and activated a heart-to-heart connection, which would allow therapist and client to have a more beneficial healing exchange.

There is a difference between eye gazing with the intent to really communicate connection and trust and see into another's soul and staring. We all know that if you lock eyes with an animal (and vice versa), then that can be viewed as an act of aggression. We see this in people as well. When someone looks deep into your eyes and it is unwelcome and you immediately feel your body and gut react, you know that the eye contact is a show of force.

Our eyes can say so much. You can tell by looking at someone's eyes if they are tired, depressed, happy, hurting, seeking, or smiling. Our eyes can communicate more than just emotions. Eyes allow us to see our outer world, to connect with our body senses, and create an exchange between how we perceive, what we are perceiving, and how we choose to receive that exchange.

Interaction with others while holding eye contact allows a more vulnerable connection. Our world has become hyper-focused on building connections with a screen between us. Sitting and really talking to someone while allowing eye contact is becoming a rare yet beautiful act.

Years ago, I was invited to be a guest speaker at a Wild Women's Symposium.

As a presenter, I was welcome to attend the other presentations. Tantra has always interested me, but being in a somewhat subdued sexual marriage for two decades didn't really allow me much room to explore tantra. When I saw that one of the presenters was doing a lecture on tantra, I jumped at the opportunity.

Tantra acknowledges that

"when you truly make love, you become god and goddess, connecting with the sacred and merging with divine light. You recreate infinity and become the boundless."

Sirona Knight.

*Tantra – a 3,000–5,000-year-old philosophy with bases in Hinduism and Buddhism allows one to deeply connect with their own energy, with the ultimate goal of achieving spiritual enlightenment."*
(https://sexualhealthalliance.com/nymphomedia-blog/tantric-eye-gazing)

When I entered the dimly lit room, I saw two beautiful women at the front, sitting cross-legged facing each other. An elaborate altar was placed behind them featuring red glowing candles in gold embossed holders. They began their presentation with eye gazing. No explanation or introduction – simply two individuals gazing into each other's eyes.

As an observer, it was a beautiful and vulnerable thing to witness. For me, I felt like I was intruding on a very intimate experience, which I feel was their intention. Eye contact between two lovers engaging in a sexual exchange is just that – vulnerable, powerful, and beautiful.

My sexual awakening post-divorce was intentional. It was vital! For 24 years my body had only known the touch of one person, with the exception of a summer where we attempted an open marriage by inviting another woman into the bedroom. No other man had kissed me or held me in a lover's embrace.

Being newly single and hell-bent on embracing my 'ho phase', as my adult children taunted me, I connected with a couple of lovers. Seeing as sex is a very intimate and personal experience that I had quite a few nerves and self-doubts to work through, and I was not ready to just jump into bed with anyone.

Choosing to engage in this kind of exchange with people I was familiar with and felt safe with was key to overcoming my insecurities. Trust was another key. When you look into someone's eyes, your body has a reaction. When you look into a lover's eyes, that reaction is quite different.

My first sexual experience after divorce was with a friend. We both had a few nerves about moving forward as friends to lovers. Our exchange began with eye contact. As if our eyes were asking each other, "Can we really do this? Do you feel safe?" Even during a sexual exchange, how often does one stop and check in with their lover with just their eyes?

As my dating life erupted and intimate exchanges became more of an experience of liberation, my sexual encounters shifted, and my intention with each experience also shifted. I became more and more aware of how our communication from table to bed involved eye contact.

My present lover and partner was a stranger to me until we locked eyes across the room. My body literally sucked in air, and I gasped with just a look of our eyes. Up until now, I had never been looked at with such intensity. This man speaks volumes with just his eyes. There was a brief introduction and then interruption as the man between us kept blocking our eye lock and interjecting his energy to himself and his chatter. Distracting, but still we maintained eye contact.

During sex, how often are your eyes closed? My lover maintains eye contact, watching constantly how our bodies move and connect with each other. In the early days, we had discussions on why my eyes were usually closed. This question was posed from a place of concern and deep intimacy. He wanted to know with sincerity. He cared.

This was a question that I would sit with and ponder during my self-reflection and personal healing. Why do I close my eyes?

Tantra eye gazing is the intense locking of eyes while sexually connected. No body movement, simply the eyes conveying and stimulating the connection. It is a very powerful energetic exchange and one that now adds a vital increase in awakening pleasure between both partners if it is allowed. It is staring into each other's eyes and seeing the pupils dilate, slowing things down and really allowing that tether between bodies to activate – not just the genitals but the heart.

Freya is well-known for her sexual prowess, but she is also known as being the one who speaks without words. Her body expressions and the way she carries herself, the way she sits on her throne, and the way she dances all speak volumes. She is a force unto herself, and I feel that is why she is so adored and cherished, not just by women but by anyone seeking a mirror of liberation and freedom, and one who can do, say, and be who they want to be. Freya is whole unto herself, and always her full self.

In my quest to awaken myself on deeper, more engaging, and liberated levels, facing fears and insecurities and exposing my vulnerabilities to not just myself but also to those I connected with in the bedroom and outside of the bedroom was essential. So, to answer the question, "Why do I close my eyes?" I had to really sit with my past and present and reformat my future.

Growing up in Utah, which is a fairly sheltered state due to the predominant religion, sex is a taboo topic. Young girls in the Church of the Latter-Day Saints (Mormons) are taught that sex is NOT for their pleasure, that it is for the sole purpose of reproduction. Growing up in this church, the common theme that I picked up on was that my body was shameful, something to be kept hidden, and my body was not for me but for my future husband and his pleasure.

Being spoon-fed this dogma from the ages of five to fifteen instilled in me a rejection and repulsion for my physical body, which would lead to multiple eating disorders, and once sixteen arrived, it projected me into open rebellion – a rebellion that would consist of using sex as a weapon against the current societal norms of my surroundings. A rebellion that would challenge me to use my body for my pleasure when and with whomever I wanted.

However, being young, inexperienced, and naïve, this rebellion didn't propel me forward; it actually anchored me deeper into stereotypical gender roles, eating disorders, and self-harming beliefs. One of which is being mother and, when my daughter turned two, as a single parent, society won again with its overwhelming pressure that every child needs two parents, and I thus entered the role of wife.

During my post-divorce explorations, while sitting with this question, I realized that the reason my eyes were closed was that I was not ready to see myself as a sexually awakened priestess of my body, bedroom, and pleasure.

I was not ready to see my body being appreciated, serviced, and connecting with someone who actually respected me. I kept my eyes closed partly because I didn't feel like I was deserving.

There was still some lingering shame from my youth, resentment from my marriage, and apprehension of where this new lifestyle would take me in the future.

Intense transformations create intense reactions within one's psyche and one's physical realm. Divorce for me was the ultimate act to rebel against society and really force myself into owning my full self without any kind of attachment to anyone else.

My body, being liberated from these tethers, decided to shed almost 50 pounds within three months with no change in diet, no exercise, and no effort. On reflection, my body was inflamed, and I was hiding myself under pounds of fat which were no longer needed. Those extra pounds were not going to serve me on my quest to expose my full self. Losing unhealthy weight is a big confidence boost!

A dear, respected high priestess friend would later point out to me that through my entire marriage I was seeking security. I was doing anything in my power to physically create a secure space, because my soul knew I was anything but secure.

In an effort to really **see** myself as the sexual priestess, I spent time naked in front of a large mirror every day, really learning to see and love my body. As an avid yoga practitioner, my daily routine consists of two 20-minute sessions – once in the morning and once before I go to bed. Moving through these yoga sessions naked allowed me to see how my body moves, how my muscles flex with each pose, and how my body really is unique to me. When I was actively training my coven students, I would often encourage them to do jumping jacks naked in front of a mirror as a way of embracing one's body in a humorous way. This devotion of yoga was different; it was more of a spiritual, slowed-down, and observed activation.

Once an individual can really see themselves fully naked and vulnerable in compromising positions, then the doorway to keeping one's eyes open during intimate connection with another is opened. Not only was I willing to see my own body respond and connect physically with a partner, but I also became increasingly intrigued by my lover's body on a visceral and visual level.

While moving through the question of keeping one's eyes open and channeling a deity such as Freya, the question shifted to, "Would Freya keep her eyes closed during sex?" The answer is an adamant NO! Can you imagine Freya crawling under the covers, ashamed of her body, clenching her eyes shut as she and her lover connected?

If our eyes are the window to our soul when we engage with another in such a powerful exchange, then we should be looking into each other's eyes as if we are challenging each other on a battlefield. After all, stripping off our armor is giving our partner(s) permission to do the same, expose their vulnerabilities, and really welcome intimacy.

We should be willing to dive deep into each other's psyche while we dive deep into each other physically.

> *"Freya was married to Odr, who often went away on his travels, journeys across the sea, and explorations that took him away from her for long periods of time. On one such journey, he did not return. Heartbroken, she went to sea, pleading and begging for her love to return to her. She began to sob, expressing her sorrows, for she knew that he would not be coming home. As her tears hit the water, they turned into stones of amber."*

The irony with this myth is that my lover is a sailor. When we met, I knew that he would be leaving for offshore work, but I had no idea just what that meant. It was two weeks after we had connected that I drove an hour to the airport to see him off, holding his hands while we took advantage of each minute we had left, then kissing him goodbye and watching him walk through the security gate and our relationship venturing into what I call 'limbo' and the unknown.

Watching someone you love (and I loved him immediately) leave for an unknown amount of time creates a spiral within. In the past seven months, I have seen him off four times, and each time I sob as Freya did. There is a *home* that forms between two people when they are deep in the throes of love. Having that home stretch with distance, oftentimes unpredictable communication, and the limbo of how as a couple you move forward when there is quite literally an ocean between you is difficult.

Tears are sacred! They are an expression of what the heart longs to say but words fail to convey the depth of.

Each time my love leaves, my tears flow heavy because we are once again having to halt our progression as a couple and dive into our own personal journeys. It is both beautiful and tragic. Each time he leaves, my tears flow just as heavily. Our love bubble stretches, and that all-too-familiar limbo creeps in.

To love so profoundly and to mourn so intensely is a different kind of wave that some of us will never have the opportunity to ride. Some of us will luckily ride that wave and will propel ourselves into embracing every moment we do have together because we know that love is rare.

Every time we bid farewell, say goodbye, or send a loved one away on a holiday or work trip, we risk losing them. It is the nature of being alive; we all meet the same ending. One would think that by simply knowing this reality, we would hold precious each moment that we have together and send each other off right! But as humans we are arrogant and often shelve for another day what we should hold on tight to.

One can imagine the tears shed as Freya went to the waters each day and waited for some sign that her love had returned. It is a mourning that every person has felt in one way or another. To watch her tears of sorrow, love, and hopelessness fall into the waters – it is no wonder they were said to turn into amber. Her love was literally and figuratively becoming immortal.

## HEALING ATTRIBUTES OF AMBER

Amber is fossilized tree sap that forms when the resin of pine and fir trees hardens. The resin falls to the ground, where it begins to slowly harden in moist areas such as riverbeds and the seabed. This process is called polymerization, and it takes millions of years.

Most amber is found on or around the shores of the Baltic Sea, ranging across Russia, Poland, Southern Sweden, Northern Germany, Latvia, and Lithuania. In the United States, amber can be found in Arkansas, New Jersey, Texas, Montana, Tennessee, New Mexico, and California, to list a few.

Because amber is fossilized tree sap that typically contains plants or insects preserved within it, many people (including the ancient civilizations) believe that it possesses healing and spiritual properties.

Most modern-day practitioners, crystal enthusiasts, New Age healers, witches, folk-crafters, and spiritualists use, wear, or display amber for its healing properties. As an individual practitioner, I typically will wear amber as enlightened jewelry to assist me in whatever particular healing I am activating at the time. For example, while writing this book, I wore a small pendant of amber around my neck for many weeks while I was percolating the concept and intention.

Amber has a very calming effect on those who choose to wear it, which is why you often see teething necklaces worn by babies and toddlers made of amber. Amber has been known to soothe the woes of teething due to its succinic acid compounds that are believed to have an analgesic effect that warms the skin, reducing the pain of teething. It is worth noting that there is no scientific proof that amber teething necklaces actually work. Much like there is no scientific evidence to support that any stone or crystal can create a specific remedy.

It is safe to say that *belief* in something activating healing is what really activates the healing. A placebo? Most likely. There is a power in amber that is intriguing. So much so that the movie *Jurassic Park* based its entire plot on the alchemist process of cloning dinosaurs using their ancient DNA found in the blood-sucking insects that were preserved in amber.

Sirona Knight, in her book *Love, Sex and Magick*, describes amber as a tree sap called the 'wet jewel' which activates the creative fire within – good for grounding and centering, and healing and harmonizing female and male energies.

> "Amber has also been used, historically, as a talisman for courage and self-confidence, and was thought to bring good luck to warriors in battle. In some cultures, amber symbolizes the renewal of marriage vows and is used to assure promises. It is worn by elders as a symbol of their endurance and wisdom." (www.firemountaingems)

Our eyes are not just windows into our souls – they are blueprints of our past, present, and future. Our eyes hold the answers that medical professionals spend far too much time performing numerous tests to discover. If we just take the time to really see into each other's eyes, we can learn so much!

> "The only thing worse than being blind is having sight but no vision."
>
> Helen Keller

## IRIDOLOGY CHART

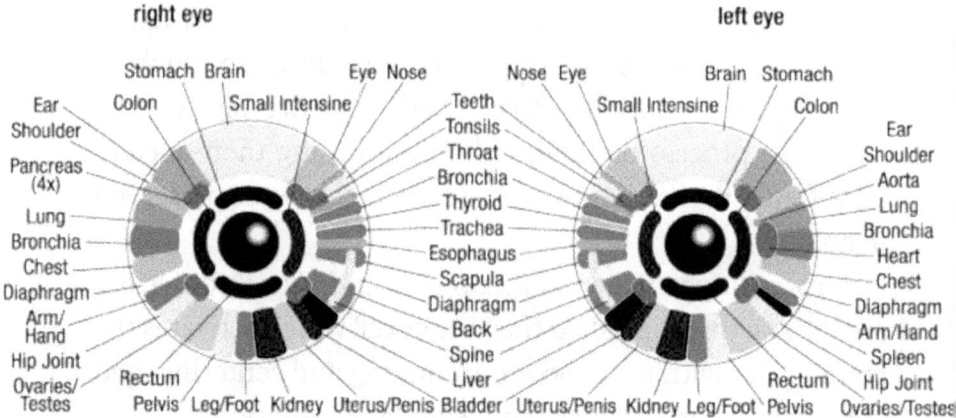

right eye

left eye

"*Iridology is the scientific study of the iris – the colored part of the eye. The iris reveals physiological conditions, psychological health risks, challenges, and/or strengths of various organs and personality traits. Iridology helps us get an understanding of your past, present, and potential future health conditions by assessing the condition of the various systems in your body. It also reveals your genetic predispositions and toxic accumulations in the various parts of your body.*"

(https://milestheeyeguy.com/iridology/)

Iridology dates back to the early Egyptians and Babylonians. In the 17th, 18th, and 19th centuries, more and more researchers began to heavily study the connection of the eyes with the workings of the body and internal organs.

Rather than treating just the symptoms, iridology addresses the entire body structure and individual, providing an economical way to maintain health free from invasive methods. Gazing into one's eyes, the individual's body and soul, offers a blueprint. How often do we really study each other's eyes?

When you go to a doctor or health care provider, do they even look at you, or are they simply prepared to offer you medicine to cure your symptoms?

When you take time to really engage in eye contact, you can really see into one's soul. You can see sorrow, exhaustion, excitement, fear, and so much more. Our eyes offer us the depth to really journey together in this chaos called life, but how often do we really invest in this kind of intense connection?

When we sit down and talk with each other, are we simply moving our mouths and going through the process of non-active listening? Or are we sitting face-to-face, maintaining eye contact, and really allowing each other time to convey our feelings while we simply sit, observe, and hear?

Maintaining eye contact with a lover is crucial. When we really gaze into each other's eyes, we invite a soulful exchange, and for just a few moments we journey into and with each other on a next-level plane. In essence, we bring our lover's soul within us.

## AN EXERCISE FOR LOVERS

Turn off your phones and step away from distractions. Sit face-to-face and really look into each other's eyes. Allow yourselves to really see each other's pupils as they will naturally dilate. Do this for at least three dilations. Next, ask each other a very personal question and just allow a response. But do not respond once they have answered; simply hold their words sacred in your heart as you continue to see into each other.

## QUESTIONS TO PONDER

- Do you see yourself?
- Do you see your lover as divine and sacred?
- Do you see yourself as divine and sacred?
- Are you making love with intention or simply seeking a physical release?
- How do you perceive yourself as a lover?
- What are your strengths and weaknesses?
- Do you love yourself?

In order to really embrace your life and share it with another, whether as a companion, casual friend, or lover, you need to be able to see yourself – your full self! If you cannot stare into the depths of your soul, sit with your depth, and see into the window of your inner knowing, then who can?

If we do not know ourselves, then we shut off our essence and create an existence where no one else can know us either. What then is the point? If we cannot take time to really see into another and allow their truths to surface on every level, then why are we wasting their time and ours? To truly know someone and see into their windows, we have to start with ourselves!

CHAPTER FOUR

# Embracing Death

ᚠ

Every new beginning is preceded by an ending. When we choose to transform ourselves, it often stems from a catalyst that has forced us to see with our amber eyes that something was not working. My role as wife needed to die! I needed to kill the wife.

When we look at the Death card in the tarot deck, most people automatically assume that something, even themselves, is going to die. This is true in a manner of speaking. Tarot-like deity work is a mirror that reflects to us things we need to see and acknowledge in our lives in order to move forward.

Embracing death was something that I needed to do. What part of myself needed to die, and how quickly could I 'kill the beast?' Anytime we anchor into a role that society has defined, we need to ask ourselves why. For me, I consciously chose the role of wife, but I chose it for the wrong reasons. My divorce was, after all, severing that role of wife.

Being someone's legal property was not something that I initially wanted to be; it was something that I thought would protect me and my daughter. Taking on someone's last name and eradicating the name and lineage I was born with was something I hadn't given much thought – it was just something you did.

Yet, now that I was faced with the choice to reclaim my previous last name or keep my married name, I jumped at the opportunity to change my name back. It was beyond liberating! After all, I had married into a horrible family that never accepted me for me. Representing their lineage was a weight I was happy to shed.

Killing that connection to his family was like taking flight. Not only did I change my last name, but I also changed my first name to a name I had been going by for over a decade. Both these steps were easy steps to take in killing the past me and helping me to rebirth the me that I had been hiding for all these years.

Rebirth, like birth, is messy! It was time to go a bit deeper into embracing death and bringing my full self through the birth canal and into this realm of my current existence. If you have ever moved through a rebirthing, then you know just how tumultuous it can be. Like the Death card, you have to call the reaper and allow things to be cut!

The Death card and Tower card go hand in hand. They make good partners, so to speak. In order to really embrace the essence of death, one has to let everything they once thought was safe and comfortable crumble and fall, brick by brick, stone by stone, until there is nothing left but an empty foundation.

That foundation is me! Throughout my marriage I had crafted a castle of my own delusions. After all, no one forced me to get married, so I said yes. No one demanded that I stay tethered in an unhealthy, toxic, abusive relationship, other than my own insecurities, self-doubts and ego. Strip away all that debris, and I was the one left standing, facing Freya in a ritual circle completely unclothed, ready to embrace new beginnings and ready to kill the creature of my own crafting.

As a feminist, I have struggled with the role and societal definition of wife since I first said "I do." A part of me knew that I was not getting married to a divine masculine that would allow me my wildness. He wanted to possess me and control me, shape me into a version that would serve his role in society and weaken mine. Property and a trophy were what I became.

Can a person ever truly be bound and owned? Yes and no. While I remained with him for over two decades, I fought back plenty. Divorce required no fight as we both filled out paperwork together and we both signed and moved onwards separately together.

Energetically, though, I had some fighting to do within myself.

Guttural tears are a force that tears one apart from the inside out – a deeper kind of purge. When the end actually hit me on a spiritual and energetic level, I vividly remember standing up and walking from the backyard into the house, where I collapsed on the bathroom floor. I cried. I cried for seven hours straight! It was as if a clawed hand had reached down into my throat and was scraping my body from the inside out. Ripping apart everything I once thought was safe and creating a clean, blank surface to rebuild on.

Power! To gut one's self is to kill oneself and embrace death. So many parts of me died that night on the bathroom floor, and I did the killing. Along with the killing came my reclaiming. Never again would I allow myself to be owned or controlled or let my worth be deemed by someone else.

As I lay there on the bathroom floor, exhausted, snot running down my face, eyes puffy and swollen, I was reminded of the selkie.

In Celtic, Irish, Scottish, and, yes, Norse mythology, there are stories of selkie women. Women who are seal first and human second. They are known to be at home in the wilds of the ocean, safe in the unknown depths and exhibiting wild freedom. Yet every now and then they surface and take off their seal skins and dance naked as wild women upon the land.

The stories go on to tell that men know of these wild women and want to possess them, owning a bit of wild nature for themselves. So they hide, wait, and watch until the women are engrossed in their frolicking on land, and then they steal their seal skins. For, once their skins are taken, selkie women cannot return to their home within the waters – they are bound, tethered, and captured.

In this weakened and vulnerable state she becomes his property, his pet, so to speak. A marriage then follows, and typically children. On the outside, it would appear that now this family is complete. Happy husband, adorable children, and a beautiful and devoted 'wife.' There is no escaping; unless the selkie finds her hidden and kept seal skin, she is bound and owned, she is nothing but property.

As I lay there on the bathroom floor, purging my old life, I could energetically see something crumpled, disposed of, and rejected lying upon the floor, not far from where I was. Divorce is an uncoupling; it takes two people, two people rejecting what they thought was once worthy and realizing that they were both wrong. My skin had not been found or given back – it was there the entire time; I just wasn't wearing it!

Before I could fully put myself together, I had to once again move through a different kind of ceremony – not a cutting, but a drowning, a death. While my cord cutting consisted of fire, this death ceremony would require water!

## SELKIE RIVER ACTIVATION

Saturday, July 27th. Five other women (who were also healing from and moving through tumultuous energetic rebirths) joined me at the river. We walked from the bridge down to the base of a waterfall, where there was a large pool of water that we could easily stand waist-deep in.

Before we began, we circled, hand in hand, our feet standing in the shallow part of the flowing waters. We shared our 'ah-ha!' moments – those moments that fully shattered us into individual realization that what once was was no more. Many tears of both sorrow and rage were

48

shared. In the center of our circle upon a stone sat a small cast iron cauldron burning juniper berries and mugwort, blessing us with sacred smoke as we released and let go before moving deeper into the water.

Once every woman had shared, we closed our eyes and went back to that pivotal moment, where there was a split, a shattering, and we envisioned our broken, crumpled selves like discarded clothing lying in a heap. We then began the process of picking that part of ourselves back up and slowly putting our broken, torn, and tattered skin back on.

It was powerful, to say the least. To stand in a circle of women, all unique but moving through their own rebirths. Once our soul skins were put back on, we moved into the water where we fully submerged – a kind of baptism, so to speak. The only difference was that we were not promising our souls or salvation to any god; we were in this flowing water, acting as our own gods – taking back what we gave away and vowing to never do so again. Liberation and freedom erupted in that river as we splashed, laughed, and played like seals.

Moving through a rebirthing of one's soul and one's life is a day-to-day challenge in asserting one's worth and vowing to not go backwards and repeat the past. This takes motivated dedication. It wasn't going to be enough to simply go into the river!

Daily forward momentum requires boundaries. Asserting boundaries with people in one's life who are not used to these boundaries can be a new kind of challenge. It can be done, though. The saying 'hold the line' is very applicable.

In killing the wife, I had to be very specific. Was I, after all, vowing to never marry again? NO! I was simply killing the wife that drowned herself in a toxic marriage. With that version of myself dead and buried, and the real me reborn, a clean slate was created. Moving forward meant not only holding boundaries for myself but also for others that would come into my life.

After all, hindsight is an incredible teacher, and when we look back at attributes in relationships that created toxicity, pain, and heartache, we can clearly define what worked and what didn't. For me, it was simple. I made another list. This list spelled out the attributes that I wanted in a partner, rather than being hyper-focused on what I didn't want.

Gratitude helped me create a more fluid forward momentum, and each day I began with expressing how grateful I was in precise detail and just what kind of partner I was manifesting. This also was applied to what kind of friends and personal health transformation I was embodying.

When we speak as if we already have what we seek, then we shift the energetic flow, and the universe responds by giving us these gifts. Trusting universal timing is also a big part of rebirthing. When we as humans can get out of our own way and stop trying to micromanage the end results, then we move into a state of being fully present, which is magic incarnate.

Cutting tethers and drowning one's past are essential and worthy deaths. The feeling of liberation is amazing! Throughout my divorce, my mantra became "Happy is a vibe!" In so many ways my life had shifted, and what most people thought would create turmoil actually created the opposite. I became elated! Roles that I had allowed myself to be consumed by were finally released!

Happiness became not just a concept out of my grasp but my day-to-day reality. Each day I was waking up living my fullest life for me, because I finally was capable of and willing to see that my happiness mattered the most! It is NOT selfish to live one's life for oneself – it is vital!

Killing roles and parts of ourselves that no longer serve us in a healthy and positive way – roles that have consumed and devoured one's ability to truly be happy – is an act of rebellion and survival. If this is our one big grand life, then why do we give it up in the pursuit of making others happy?

For two decades, I was living for my children and attempting to live up to society's projection of how a 'good wife' should be, look, and act. Two decades is a very long time to waste living for anyone but myself. Self-awareness is another big key in moving through and activating death.

Sooner, hopefully, rather than later, as individuals we all recognize that there are relationships, situations, and circumstances that will require a death, an ending, in order to establish a re-do, new beginning, and rebirth.

As an avid reader of the tarot and a teacher to those new to the cards, I always advise my clients to sit with a card, especially if it is one from the Major Arcana. Sit with the card, look at the symbolism, and really allow a connection between those symbols to highlight what is currently happening in your life.

Here in Utah, tarot cards have a somewhat humorous reputation. Frequent customers in my area avoid the metaphysical, New Age, and tarot sections as if there is a plague they might catch. Tarot cards are linked with the occult, and here in this almost primarily Christian state, the occult is deemed *evil and of the devil*.

How pieces of paper with lovely artwork on them can hold such dark power is a mystery to me. So, I do my best to educate and raise awareness of the history of tarot and ultimately how any kind of supernatural power doesn't come from the cards but rather from the person using them. We as humans attach energy to the cards. We give them power when in actuality they hold none.

When the Death card kept showing up for me in my daily devotional card pulls, I took note and reassured myself that I was on the right path. For me, the cards are simply mirrors of the energy that I am creating for myself on a day-to-day basis. They offer reassurance, direction, and insight, if I, the reader, am willing to sit with them and ultimately sit with myself and allow the symbols to connect as a bridge with myself and the universe.

A metaphorical ending that allows us to see
the possibility of new beginnings.
All good things must come to an end!
We die each day, in one way or another.
To die is to live, again and again!

When I teach tarot, I ask that each student spend one day with one card in the Major Arcana and really get to know that card as if they were getting to know a new potential friend. The Major Arcana cards represent life cards – where we are at the present moment in our lives. They are the mirrors of our soul journey and inner archetypes.

Sitting with the Death card can be a struggle because we have been programmed to fear endings rather than embrace them. When you begin to develop a new relationship with a card, you will see that certain symbols stand out to you more than to others. This happens because we are individuals and our lives are individual. While there are basic meanings attached to each card, we as the reader can and do take those meanings deeper, because we apply them to ourselves.

When I sat with the Death card, what stood out to me was the white horse. A white horse can mean many things, but to me the white horse represented freedom, liberation, and a pure momentum to take me forward.

The skeleton, wearing armor yet sitting confidently, to me was the key. Spiritual armor is created by the individual. If the skeleton represents me and this death in my life, then I know that I am protected to move forward by the armor of knowledge. My past taught me, and the ability to carry those wounds as a part of me in defense rather than resentment would help in my efforts to really rebirth. Stripping down to the bones and being able to really sit with one's chosen roles and see that they are no longer applicable is a strong foundation. Being able to bare those bones, learn from them, and move onward with life, carrying those lessons and being determined to not repeat them, is transformation in action. It is birth!

The figure trampled underneath the horse was the third thing that really stood out to me. In this battlefield of life, there are going to be casualties. Did this crumpled figure represent my ex or that part of me that I had allowed to fester and be broken for two decades? For me, the trampled figure was both. My ex needed to go away! As the skeleton, I would ride over and away from him in many ways, and some days it was not pretty.

That part of me, that *wife*, those gender roles, and the feelings that came with them were really what I was trampling. She needed to die. So, as the skeleton, I would trample her. The most intense casualty in our lives is the death of ourselves from a life that we once thought was our everything.

Killing the wife was a harsh reality. There were many versions of myself in that role that were toxic, painful, and unrealistic. These were attributes that I allowed to grow and wore like a costume for far too long. That version of me was outdated and was not going to take me forward – rather, she was going to eventually be the death of my inner wild, myself as queen.

With the cord cutting, I severed the energetic tether. As selkie, I stood, bared to the bones. I picked up my crumpled, trampled self and let the waters take away the residual muck so that I could move forward reborn.

Water is life, and some waves in our storms of life are calm and gentle. When activating an energetic and spiritual death, there is no time to sit upon the surface waters and ride the calm waves. After all, transformation does not happen in the 'lazy river' of life. True and full shattering happens in the tumultuous waves that attempt to break us.

When we crash like catalysts against the old foundations of our life that once were salvation and break them apart, piece by piece, we let those waves pull us under to the depths, to that place where death awaits to bring more life and joy than we anticipated or even imagined.

Looking back at those two decades, I can see that I was sleeping in a state of denial. I had become complacent. I had settled for far less than anyone deserved, and I was scared to dive down into those deep dark places of my soul that were screaming for oxygen.

Robert Frost wrote that "the only way out is through." This phrase has stuck with me and reminded me that for far too long I was avoiding the truth. There was no unconditional love in my marriage, no passion, and no friendship. In the two decades of my life with no change, excitement, or joy, the only way out was to push through!

Avoiding the obstacles was not activating the warrior who seeks a good death. Rather, to avoid it was to feed the coward and delay my growth. Freya is the one who had the final say on which warriors fought well in battle and deserved a place at Odin's table in Valhalla. She is judge, jury, and queen.

In activating her essence and attributes as a mirror to embody this act of death, killing the wife was my ultimate act as judge, jury, and queen of my own castle! To embrace death as the only inevitable certainty is to demand that we live with purpose each and every day!

To live is to die a thousand deaths or more! We are constantly throughout our lives dying, or killing parts of ourselves that must perish in order for us to progress. Each time I bid my love farewell, and go home and cry, there is a part of codependency tendencies that must die in order for me to be able to move throughout my life as a separate entity, even though in a committed relationship.

*"To live is to die. To die is to live. To avoid death, is to avoid living."*

Sunday Adelaja

# CHAPTER FIVE

# Sacred Adornment

To adorn one's body as something sacred is a gift of acknowledgement that we give ourselves. Sadly, most people have lost the ability to see that their body is actually sacred and worthy of adornment.

How we dress reflects a personal relationship with how we view ourselves physically and emotionally. Before my divorce, I hid myself under dresses, baggy tank tops, and 40+ pounds of excess weight. My physical body was inflamed, and I was not happy. That unhappiness showed in how I carried myself, dressed, and treated my body.

Post-divorce, those excess 40+ pounds seemed to evaporate! In a span of three months, I had gone from a size 12 to a size 5. My confidence elevated, and I stopped hiding. I had always been embarrassed by my belly, and now I was more than ready to show it off! Crop tops became an everyday part of my ensemble. I was no longer in hiding, and I was ready to show the world just how confident I was.

Our solar plexus chakra, or energy focal point, is located between our navel and diaphragm. When a person has activated their self-confidence and is whole and holy in their expression of their full selves, then this chakra point is fully engaged – and it shows!

The solar plexus holds our fears, gut feelings, insecurities, stamina, and willpower. For far too long, I was afraid to leave an unhappy marriage. I denied and ignored, tucked away my gut feelings, and sank into my insecurities. All stamina and willpower had become complacent and compromised.

Not anymore! I was fully engaged in forward momentum. Cutting tethers, killing the wife, and drowning those old societal gender roles that had consumed me for far too long had liberated me on levels that words cannot describe. My attitude toward myself had drastically changed because I had chosen myself, my worth, and my happiness.

Again, happy is a vibe! When someone is truly happy, it glows like a fire from the inside out. Happiness becomes a force and a beacon for others to see, enjoy, be inspired by, and celebrate. My entire wardrobe had to shift and transform in an effort to keep up with my inner and outer transformation.

Old frumpy clothes that had been hiding who I was were no longer welcome in my dresser or my closet. Instead, I went shopping. It was fun to be fully liberated and to buy clothes that didn't have to be approved of by anyone other than myself!

Freya was known to be the most beautiful of the Norse deities. She would exude sexual confidence – pun intended, as 'exude' by definition means "to discharge (moisture or smell) slowly and steadily" – with her knowing who she was as a whole and holy individual.

This confidence, I'm certain, was intimidating to those who were lacking in their own inner knowing. While at the same time, I am sure it was inspiring. When we look to goddesses, queens, and figures in myths and legends that stand supreme, whole, and powerful as individuals, they become a powerhouse mirror that we can strive to be like, or we can be jealous of.

Jealousy is a sad emotion. It stems from insecurities, and in our modern world, we are spoon-fed the notion that jealousy is normal and accepted. This is false! We have been taught to compare and compete with each other, especially as females. When, in reality, there is nothing to compare or compete with.

As an individual who is gloriously unique and fucked-up, just like everyone else in the world, I do not wish to be like anyone else, and no one could ever be me. So there is nothing to envy, desire, or want that someone else has. As an individual, I am more than capable of obtaining everything and anything that I truly want – and that want is formulated for me. There is no hunger in me to have what my neighbors two doors down have. Nor would I want to look like anyone but me.

We are here to have a truly unique and authentic life experience. When we can stop with that jealous waste of energy, we can fully embody confidence. Looking to the old gods, we again do so for inspiration and not because we wish to become them. That would be considered somewhat sacrilegious. It has always been my belief that the gods/goddesses are mirrors that show us our own capabilities if we choose to activate them.

Dressing for the job you want is a good method of activating these mirrors. Post-divorce, I shed the adornment of being someone's property. I was no longer tethered, chained, or owned! I was free to get up each day and dress the way that I wanted to and be my full self, anytime, anywhere. I was queen of my body and castle each and every day.

## FREYA AND BRISINGAMEN

Myths, sagas, and legends will tell you that Freya the Goddess of Battle, Beauty, Sexuality, Passion, and Teacher of Seidr (ancient Norse magic of divination), wore upon her neck a torc, or powerful necklace made of gold, wielded and shaped by four dwarves: Dvalinn, Alfrik, Berlingr, and Grer. Freya, being queen unto herself, wanted this necklace. When she went to the four dwarves and offered them all her fortune for it, they refused. Freya, being frustrated, asked what she could make as an offer that would allow her to obtain this necklace if they did not want her gold. The dwarves each responded that they would happily give her the necklace if she agreed to spend one night with each of them. Freya agreed!

As a goddess known for her sexual freedom and prowess, why would she not? The selling of one's body is nothing new, especially for women. Being seen as simply an object meant for sexual pleasure is something that most people would not dispute. I like to look at Freya's decision as the opposite. She was in complete control! This was, after all, a wager that she agreed to, and she would be the one calling the shots' even though we are misled to believe otherwise. It is my belief that there is more to the story.

I do not believe that Freya, the almighty goddess of her own sexual sovereignty, simply agreed to endure one night with each dwarf just for a necklace. Let's be real, Freya is a queen who, I am positive, had men lined up waiting for her to simply acknowledge them. For her to simply give her body away for four nights in a row to four dwarves for a necklace degrades her essence, her magnitude, and her power.

It is my belief that the sagas forget to mention the details on purpose, because they were written by a man who was known to be a rumored Christian philosopher. So, naturally, he would carry into his writings those Christian wounds that depict women as being less than and only good for the sexual pleasures of men.

We need to stay realistic and remember that no one actually knows the truth of the Norse gods, because what we do have in writing was written some 200 years after the supposed dates of the events, and can we really trust who wrote these stories, myths, and sagas? The answer is NO! There are no factual historical records of ANY existence of ANY of the gods, let alone what they may or may not have done in order to obtain possession of a necklace!

Which begs us to ask ourselves, the readers, "Why do we care?" What does Freya's necklace represent to us, the individuals? That's the question we should be asking. The wearing of a torc, or half-moon-shaped metal necklace, adorned with stones and jewels that fits around one's neck, is a symbol of royalty, strength, protection, and nobility.

The torc is very common in Celtic and Nordic mythology, artwork, and stone carvings. There simply has to be some kind of power attached to something that the most important members of these tribes were found to be wearing.

Torc by definition means 'twisted metal'. The torcs found in ancient burials were simply that – metal that was twisted and too large to be worn anywhere other than around the neck. These ancient torcs date back to the Bronze Age.

To wear sacred adornments such as a torc is to announce one's status. Plain and simple! A torc was a status symbol, and as such, demanded respect. Only the most esteemed, powerful, royal, and respected would be seen wearing a torc around their neck. Especially when we consider the time and energy it would require to forge such an item.

Sacred adornment is nothing new. Kings and queens have crowns upon their heads that highlight their status amongst their colonies and kingdoms. It goes without saying that before there were head crowns, there were torcs.

Naturally, Freya, as queen of the most esteemed great hall, known for her lavish celebrations, would be adorned with such an object that would show her wealth, status, and power to those who looked up to her. This torc would appear to be one of her great treasures.

Did she have sex with four dwarves in order to obtain this necklace or torc? Sure! Maybe?! But on her terms, not theirs, for she knew what she was wagering and offering. The big question is why are we taught that she of all people or deities would lessen herself to simply an object in order to obtain an object? Is this a way for the historian to taint her status and image as a woman whole unto herself? I believe the answer is yes!

During my journey with Freya post-divorce, I wore a solid black leather cord with an amber pendant. Nothing fancy, just a piece of raw amber with a hole in it that was big enough for the leather to go through. This was my sacred adornment.

Wearing amber helped me to stay connected to Freya energy, and it reminded me of my own connection with amber as a healing ally. When we wear jewelry, we do it with purpose. There is something about each piece that we as individuals have attached a meaning to.

Modern-day practitioners of the craft often wear specific jewelry as an outward symbol of their beliefs. We have seen this in other religions as well. The wearing of religious jewelry is a sign of devotion, one's faith, and connection to the divine, as defined by the wearer.

When I was actively leading public Wiccan ceremonies, I will admit that there was a show of performative priestess work with how I dressed and adorned myself. Primarily I would dress in a way that would reflect my own inner workings with the specific deity that I would be calling in during the ceremony.

Every circle, grove, and coven has their own set way, their own dogma so to speak, and their own methods with ceremonies. Each priestess or priest incorporates their own unique authenticity while moving through these kinds of specific lineage practices. Some Wiccan traditions practice only skyclad or in the nude.

As an animist priestess, I have moved away from the three lineages I was ordained into and have created my own style – one much less performative and more spontaneous. Some that circle with me refer to me as a 'dirty priestess' because I have shelved the 'costumes' and circle – as I have in what I am wearing.

To each their own! When you do ceremony and call to the divine, as you define it, this act should be for you and for your own healing' not for others' entertainment or critique. There is no one way – there is only your way, for this is your individual practice.

Wear what you want! If you have ceremonial jewelry, then you know the personal meaning behind each piece, and that is all that matters. As humans, we have attached meaning to many different material items. This, I believe, helps us to stay connected to and display a belief in something greater than ourselves.

Every now and then, I like to go through my jewelry and ritual attire. This is a kind of transformational inventory to see just how far I have progressed and moved through my life as a day-to-day ceremony.

After my divorce, I found that there were pieces of jewelry that no longer served me or needed to take up space in my life or my future. These pieces were either gifted, buried, or tossed into a ceremonial fire.

Some of these items consisted of jewelry that was gifted to me by my now ex.

While at the time I appreciated them, now as I looked at them, they were tainted with memories that I no longer wanted to hold onto. It was time to purge and release in order to make room for new!

I filled a box with jewelry and clothing. It was liberating to *hang up my old crowns* and items that connected me to the past. My body is sacred each and every day, and I will adorn it with items and clothing that represent me, make me feel comfortable, and highlight to the outside world my authenticity. I no longer dress to impress – I dress to express me and my liberated, happy vibe!!!!!

I am certain that if Freya owned a torc that was bejeweled and showed her status as a queen and goddess, whole unto herself, she did so with pizzazz! We will never know the truth as to how she actually obtained such a necklace, or even why we have been taught that she gave herself as a sexual object in order to earn such a necklace.

Like all the myths and sagas, they are open to our own individual interpretation. Maybe her offering herself is something that we as humans can relate to, reflect on, and heal? Maybe in my marriage I offered up many parts of myself for a ring and a social status?

When we become employed, there is often a uniform that we wear to show that we are representing the company we work for. Years ago, when I worked for law enforcement, I wore a very specific uniform with a badge that showed the public my status. In marriage, we do the same. Although I had a wedding ring (and when it was placed upon my finger, it meant something; it was a promise), when that promise repeatedly was broken, that ring found a new home in the back of my drawer in my dresser, not to be worn.

Now here I sit, some nine months post-divorce, with a new ring on my finger, and this ring represents a new promise, a new relationship, a new hope, and a new beginning. While people outside of my life can visually see this new ring and formulate an opinion and make assumptions about me, the meaning behind this particular ring packs a much deeper explanation of my individual growth and progression.

After all, when we wear sacred adornments, we do so first and foremost for ourselves! Or at least we should be thinking of our own selves and our right to express ourselves outwardly in a manner that reflects how we feel inwardly. Sacred adornment should complement our own sacred devotion on a day-to-day basis!

So, wear the outfit that you have tucked away for a special occasion. Every day you are above ground is a special occasion. Put on that necklace, ring, or bracelet that you have been saving or holding off on wearing out of concern for other people's opinions.

Be the king, be the queen of your own castle, and show the world who you are. Stand whole and holy within your authenticity and let it shine! Let people talk; they will, no matter what. Let them judge. Let them question your audacity to adorn yourself as if you are sacred. Maybe, just maybe, you can be a mirror and ignite a spark and give others permission to start viewing themselves and adorning themselves as if they too are sacred.

The act of sacred adornment is a reminder each day that we see ourselves as sacred and we are taking the time to put on the airs – which means to dress and act in a way that suggests you are superior to others. Yes, this may seem arrogant, but it doesn't have to be. If you are putting on airs and investing in your physical health and wanting to remind yourself of just how sacred you are, and that comes across as arrogant to others, then they can keep their opinions to themselves.

After all, other people's opinions are really none of our business. Each of us is here to fully live and embody our unique lives as our full, fucked-up selves. If we are giving ourselves permission to do that without judgment, then we should do the same for others.

We have all had moments in our lives where we have witnessed an individual fully embodying their authenticity and not giving 'any fucks'. These people exude confidence whether they really are confident or not. They adorn themselves to express themselves, and, let's face it, we have admired them for that.

Appreciating someone and allowing others to show up as their full selves is a true form of love and it stems from our ability to do that ourselves. So, be you; other people can adjust, or they can keep their opinions to themselves.

Keep on keeping on!

CHAPTER SIX

# Taking Flight

ᚠ

Rising up as an individual that loves, accepts, and honors oneself as whole and holy can be a challenge. Especially in a society that teaches us that codependency and caring about what other people think is the norm, and we should actually take the time to consider and reflect on these outward opinions.

During my divorce, I experienced an ample number of people reaching out to express their opinions and offer me unsolicited advice and sympathies. Shutting down my social media accounts helped me in shutting up these unwelcome outsiders' perspectives.

As an animist, looking at animals as a mirror also helped. One animal I saw often during my current situation was a falcon. This was no rare event, as falcons are very common in the area where I live. Also, I believe in universal synchronicities. So, having made my call to Freya, I know that I had asked for her energy and attributes to come into my life in a manner that I would recognize them and connect them back to her.

Freya is said to possess another sacred adornment, that being a cloak made of falcon feathers, which allows her to turn herself into a falcon. We see this as a common theme in many myths, sagas, and legends. The ancient ones often possess an article of clothing that helps them transform, travel, and move beyond the realms.

The ability to shift shape is something that most humans find to be intriguing.

Were these ancient ones really capable of changing their physical form into another form, or was this more of an energetic concept, experienced within the realm of one's mind and imagination?

Can we as humans physically change our body from that of a human to an animal? I am unaware of any factual evidence that would confirm this occurrence. However, as one that often moves through shapeshifting meditations, I can say that there are many times I have traveled through my own mind in the shape of an animal.

Activating bird energy is to imagine being able to soar above the mundane problems that as muggles we often face and embrace the idea of being an observer. Bird energy is all about perspective. As a bird, can we fly up, rise above, and look down at the current issues we are dealing with and see multiple ways of maneuvering through them?

As a bird of prey, knowing when to swoop down and attack and when to keep flying are both ways to maneuver and take a firm grasp on any situation. Falcons are just that

– 'birds of prey'. They are quick when attacking, using their finely-tuned instincts to see and act. Their talons are sharp and ready to take control.

Freya of course would have a falcon cloak and have the ability to become a falcon in her life – maybe not physically, but metaphorically. As a woman whole unto herself, she would have often faced situations where that bird of prey, fight or flight, would need to come into action. Let's face it, in life we should all fine-tune our fight or flight defenses and begin to use them with more precision.

Unfortunately, we do not! We move into the ego brain and weigh up the pros and cons, we second-guess ourselves, and we often repeat mistakes, thinking that for some reason this time will be different. When we activate animal instincts, there is no room for ego, because animals do not have ego brains! They are 100% reliant upon their instincts for survival.

Upheaval in life is just part of life. Each day, while a new beginning is often filled with moments that are unexpected, at times they catch us off guard, and we enter the realm of being uncomfortable.

In the midst of winter, we had a freeze, and when I arrived home, one of the pipes was definitely not flowing. Not even giving it much thought other than panic, I rushed outside, lifted the cover on the crawlspace, and in my pajamas and bare feet, I army-crawled under the house to find the frozen pipe and hoped that it had not burst. As luck would have it, the pipe was not all the way frozen, so I rushed back in the house and hunted for tape or string – anything that I could use to bind the hot water pipe to the cold so that I could get the cold water pipe flowing.

It was six degrees outside, and here I was rushing back and forth from in the house to under the house. Panic! In the middle of winter, a frozen pipe is not something that anyone wants. Luckily, I was able to thaw the pipe quickly, and then I found a leak. Hope sank almost instantly.

Knowing that the temperature was going to drop below zero, I was defeated. I returned to the house, accepting that I had done all that I could and a plumber was the next step. After a restless night, the weather warmed up, and the next day, as I waited for the plumber to arrive, I re-evaluated my life.

Sometimes the best thing you can do in a situation like this is shift the energy and seek a different perspective. So, in the middle of January, I got out the ladder and climbed up onto the roof. While gazing out at my yard and sanctuary that was filled with 24 years of memories, hardships, and trials, and then feeling the energy of my broken house beneath me, I asked myself a hard question, "Could I fly away from it all?"

Normally in a divorce, the property is divided. We had chosen to split the house 50/50 and not sell just yet... As I stood on the roof and contemplated my future here in this house as the main caretaker, provider, and the one that would ultimately be responsible for the financial burden of all the piled-up repairs, I answered my question with a very confident "YES!"

When we disconnect and seek higher ground, we embrace birdlike energy, and we can really take time to reflect, contemplate, and feel the shift that comes with a changed perspective. For me, the shift felt like liberation. Once the decision was made, I felt light as if I were lifting off the ground. My worries were to become feathers, and I would use those feathers to soar elsewhere.

Freya's cloak was a very valuable tool that Loki was known to borrow, along with the other Aesir. I liken this to Harry Potter's cloak of invisibility – a coveted, magical garment that can bestow the wearer with shapeshifting powers.

Who wouldn't want to be a bird of prey for a day? To fly upwards into the sky and look down below and see one's life through the lenses of a bird? It would be quite the experience. When you can look down at something in your life with a new perspective, you can really see just how small the issue really is or can be made out to be.

Anytime you seek a new perspective, you include reflection. Sometimes, when you are looking down upon your life, it is nice to see and remember just how much you have actually accomplished and conquered.

> "In a bird's-eye view, you tend to survey everything and decide on a particular point; then you swoop down and pick it up.
> In a worm's-eye view, you don't have that advantage of looking at everything."
>
> Muhammad Yunus

When we activate a bird's-eye view, it involves more than just seeing the issues one is currently facing. This form of shifting perspective should also include observing one's thoughts and chosen emotions. In essence, one is watching one's own mind.

Accountability is also an excellent form of shifting. When we can own our emotions without blame, we can really take flight and move forward with quick momentum.

'Metacognition' – a term often used by therapists – is "the act of awareness and understanding of one's own thought processes." It is defined as "the capacity to reflect on, evaluate, and control cognitive processes such as decision-making, memory, and perception." One activity that therapists who use metacognition in their sessions use is to apply a bird's-eye view. This practice is often called thinking about thinking (the www.cambridgeinternational.org/images/272307-metacognition.pdf).

How often do we as humans take time to really reflect on and evaluate our past decisions and our future opportunities? Standing on the roof, looking down at my past, offered me a new kind of sight – a vision and a reminder of everything that I had accomplished and everything I was now willing to fly away from and give up.

Once again, Freya was giving me the opportunity to be queen and move in a new direction. She was encouraging me to put on a feathered cloak and see that I can take flight towards something new and exciting. But my wings would never soar if I was tethered to my past.

In my first book, *Animals as Gods*, I dove into the art of shifting perspective through shapeshifting with falcon. Since that book was published, I have had many opportunities to fly side-by-side with friends and clients as they journeyed through this expansion. It is exhilarating to witness individuals take back their power and shift from victimhood to power.

When I moved in with my love back in December of 2024, we were both unaware of what would transform within the neighborhood. It soon became apparent that our relationship was not liked. It is very interesting to experience people interjecting themselves into others' lives out of jealousy and then creating malice to project their envy.

We soon fell under attack of stalking and harassment, which would later include local law enforcement becoming involved. What we thought was going to be our 'forever home' soon became an unsafe space, one that we would have to move out of. Throughout the seven-month ordeal, we remained vigilant as king and queen of our castle. Despite having injunctions filed against us and on our behalf, we pushed forward.

Many mornings we would sit out front and observe the neighborhood while we cuddled up with each other, shared our dreams, laughed, and listened to our music.

Observation is a valuable tool and an act of allowing perspectives to surface. It became such a frustration to even question the motives being thrust at us, but also incredibly disheartening that people would take so much time and energy out of their lives to try and make one couple who were simply minding their own business unhappy.

Taking flight would take on a whole new meaning. There is only so much anxiety one can handle, and mid-August it became clear that we were no longer safe living in our own home. We made the decision to list it for sale with an agent and begin the sad and stressful process of packing up our things and relocating.

Freya was a pivotal energy in our fleeing. Each day, I would stand at my altar and call to Freya for strength, insight, and queenly poise. Each day, I would envision her wings extending from my arms, allowing me to rise up and see above and beyond the possibilities and opportunities just over the horizon, beyond this fuckery.

# CHAPTER SEVEN

# Prowess & Bravery

ᚠ

Prowess by definition means "to possess a skill or expertise in a particular activity or field." In a position of power such as a king or queen, these skills are taught at a very young age. What we forget is that we too have been taught how to be kings and queens in our lives. Or maybe we should have been taught these skills more? What we do possess is the ability to learn and become experts.

When we look at Freya as a mirror of what we as mere humans are more than capable of embodying, we tend to see her, more often than not, as a lover of many.

Is that her only superpower?

With Odin and Thor being the top-tier influential deities in Norse mythology, Freya is often third on the list. She was and still is loved, adored, worshipped, and idolized. She was the most desired being in all the Nine Worlds. Still today we desire to be like her, we crave to obtain her prowess – but her prowess in what?

First and foremost, she is the goddess that quite literally is desire. As one whose name means 'lady', she is not only physically beautiful, but she is also captivating and alluring in her elegance, strength, bravery, and, let's face it, her independence. She stands supreme as a sovereign queen of her own self.

When we think of someone so enticing and breathtaking, we don't always see the armor and the sword, or hear the battle cry. Freya was not just a figure to look at, she was frightening on the battlefield. She was a fierce warrior! It is rumored that she alone killed half the Aesir troops.

Freya was the queen with no king – a woman so powerful that every man and woman craved her attention and affection. She is the ideal balance of strength and beauty. Throughout history, all over the world, we see queens from all pantheons that were described as both beautiful and powerful – true queens that possessed the prowess to fight in battles, captivate their enemies, and rule their kingdoms, oftentimes as widows.

Divorce taught me many things about myself. Mostly, I learned what I was truly capable of and which battles I was willing to fight and which battles were no longer mine. Standing firm in my independence meant facing not just the scrutiny of those who did not fully understand the situation, but I also faced appreciation and admiration.

To be a queen means to mirror prowess to everyone at all times. Queens are always being watched and observed. Freya fought; she won the battle for Odin, earned his respect, and thus the people's devotion. She also bewitched and allured with her outward beauty and, I am sure, her physical strength.

Freya's ultimate prowess lies in her power of persuasion. One can assume that very few, if any, resisted her charms or orders, whether they be in the bedroom or on the field of battle.

When we think of the prowess that a queen must possess, the list is long! A queen should be kind, regal, generous, confident, brave, bold, honest, gracious, decisive, committed, wise, thoughtful, strong, loyal, and so on.

When you sit with yourself and take inventory of who you are, can you create a list that highlights what kind of king or queen you are in your own inner kingdom?

After all, your home is your castle, and your family is your kingdom.

Post-divorce, I sat with pen and paper and made many lists. Looking back, I was in many ways a decent queen, but I was not living up to my fullest potential. I had not fine-tuned any prowess worth exuding, let alone having people see. However, I did create a list of what kind of queen I was ready to be, and that list was long! That list was worthy, and that list was doable.

Queens and kings with prowess are not just handed a silver spoon. They have invested time, energy, blood, sweat, and tears into learning skills that equate to expertise in their particular field.

Freya was loved by all. She was depicted in the myths and numerous legends as being loving, kind, generous, and attractive. In this modern world where we look to myths as metaphors and lessons, rather than facts and blueprints, we can develop an understanding that with this love, kindness, and generosity that Freya possessed, she must also have had those feelings towards herself.

To really be able to love someone, you need to really love yourself. This is a battle of its own. Society has taught us that on some levels self-love is selfish. The number-one derogatory name I was called following my divorce was 'selfish'.

Was it selfish of me to choose me and my happiness? NO! But to those who saw me as only giving and taking care of everyone around me, the sudden change probably seemed out of character and shocking.

To really be able to offer kindness, one needs to be kind to oneself. We need to formulate a barometer that registers to us what kindness feels like so that we can outwardly offer that to others. We have to know, on some level, what receiving kindness does to our hearts and souls.

To be generous, one must be generous to oneself. There is a pattern. All change must start within. There is no genuine love, kindness, or generosity that does not happen inside for the individual first.

Freya taught me that throughout this entire process of embracing death and shapeshifting into the new beginning of rebirth, I needed to start by taking care of my own needs. I needed to be kind, generous, and loving to me….for once!

The process was a bit unnerving in the beginning. For 24 years, I had prowess in being less than my spouse. This was a skill that I had become an expert in. His needs, and my children's needs, his wants, their wants, and his career – all of these things came first. My needs were inconsequential and certainly not vital. I had consumed the poison that society had fed me in this patriarchal state, and I had drowned the feminist inside that was screaming.

In order to shapeshift and reclaim my selkie skin, I started to say no to those who had needed me for so many years and started to say yes to my needs. My days began with me and my needs, first and foremost. A weekly date night with myself became a different kind of ritual, much to the disapproval of many. Believe me, there were many that openly disapproved of my behavior.

My first date night consisted of going to the local dive bar for karaoke. I put on my tightest black dress and elegant vintage shoes, grabbed my purse, and ventured out after nine in the evening – which was unheard of! Typically, I'd have had three glasses of wine and a book in hand by this time. But that person who hid behind the pages and sipped fermented grape juice was not going to ruin my date night with myself.

Out the door I went! Karaoke nights tend to have their crowd of regulars, and I was new to the crowd. My giving 'no fucks' was mirrored back by a small group of what I fondly call 'misfits'. Instantly, there was a connection and camaraderie filled with laughter, dancing, singing, and zero judgment.

In the beginning of establishing one's prowess, there needs to be bravery.

Stepping out into the public, recently single, entering a bar that my ex was known to frequent, and having zero friends forced me to be brave.

Bravery by definition means "to exhibit courageous behavior and/or character." Stepping out into the unknown required some bravery. Freya was a warrior – she was unabashedly brave! Throughout my post-divorce period, her attributes would move through me as me in a parallel manner.

Freya is a lioness stalking every inch of her kingdom in a manner to protect and love. Lions are brave, courageous, strong, and powerful. After all, the male lion is referred to as the king of the jungle, so naturally his mate would be the queen of the jungle. If you have watched a lioness move, you will know that they move with grace, poise, and precision.

Felines in general move in such a way that they possess their surroundings. They are sure-footed, quick, and agile. Felines are also, for the most part, very confident and capable of fending for themselves.

Is it any wonder that Freya rides in a chariot pulled by two large male cats? In an article on the norsecraft.com website, these two cats are described as "companions to Freya; they embody her multifaceted nature, representing both the wild, untamed aspects of the natural world and the nurturing, protective qualities of a mother goddess. In Norse society, cats were also believed to possess magical powers, capable of seeing in the dark and warding off evil spirits. This mystical aura further enhances their connection to Freya, elevating them to the status of divine guardians and companions."

Spirit animals are mirror reflections of an individual's most raw, natural, primal, uninhibited, and instinctual self. When we embody these animals as mirrors, we give ourselves as humans permission to become more guttural and less ego-driven.

In the past 20 years of offering spirit animal connection activation sessions all over the country, I have become increasingly aware that feline energies are more commonly expressed in those who embody their femininity. To break it down, I have had very few masculine connections with felines as their primary spirit animal (primary being an animal that one embodies for several years, rather than a day-to-day connection).

It has also been fascinating to see that the feminine who do connect with a feline are often individuals who are comfortable with their physical and energetic surroundings on a solitary level.

Felines are typically not pack-oriented. They hunt and scavenge alone. While they may live in colonies, they are more than capable of self-survival. With the exception of lions, which do live in a group. When we think of pack-oriented animals, we often think of dogs – particularly wolves.

Shifting energetically on a very personal level from being a pack-oriented individual with wolf as my primary spirit animal was a challenge. My pack, or family structure, had divided; my children turned on me, and in preservation I had no choice but to stalk, hunt, and take control of my life in a very catlike and solitary way.

The colony or group of misfits that I embraced were all actively moving through their own individual and solitary journeys. When we gathered together, we did so as if we were a bunch of feral cats refusing to be tethered by unhealthy social norms.

A group of wild cats is often referred to as a 'destruction' or a 'colony' – the term and definition of 'destruction' referring to the need to defend one's territory, often in a destructive manner – while 'colony' refers to a group of cats that live together in close proximity for survival.

My group of misfits most certainly was both! Going out a couple times a week to dance, drink, and be feral as an individual, I embraced the definition and took it to heart – "to be in a wild state, especially after escape from captivity or domestication."

As a sovereign queen, I had in many ways escaped a form of captivity, and I was wildly against being domesticated and controlled. My prowess would be allowing myself, my full self, to surface in all aspects of my life for once, without the fear of judgement, criticism, and rejection.

Surrounding myself with like-minded individuals or feral cats was a medicine that became salvation. Throughout our lives we attract like magnets, and vice versa, people who are mirrored reflections of either the things we need to see and work on within ourselves OR things we need to see, embrace and allow to surface. My misfits were mirrors of both. My prowess became my discernment of seeing both the things I needed to work on and the things I needed to surface.

Moving through life as a solitary queen of self and owning one's fuck-ups is a huge act of bravery. To be brave is to exude a courageous character and/or behavior.

*"When life seems hard, the courageous do not lie down and accept defeat; instead, they are all the more determined to struggle for a better future."*

Queen Elizabeth II

# CHAPTER EIGHT

# Sacred Connection

**B**eing at peace and owning one's sexuality, sexual preferences, and identity has become more than just the norm in this modern world that we live in. This 'in your face' expression that was once shunned, private, and spoken of in secret is now openly displayed and encouraged. We have celebrations, parades, drag shows, fundraisers, and so much more!

With this insurgence, it has become vital to not only step into one's FULL self but to also allow space for others to do the same. For this movement, we need a deity that can mirror authenticity, passion, sovereignty, dignity, and unbridled sexuality. Thankfully we have Freya!

While we know Freya to be spoken of as a goddess of love and sacred sexuality, her necklace Brisingamen gifted her with charm, good fortune and the ability to allure, captivate, and entrance; or rather, should we say, ensnare.

Freya simply wears the necklace; it is an inanimate object that holds power like any other inanimate object does because of the one wearing it.

Freya is the one that exudes charm and beauty and possesses the magick of attraction. Is this manipulation? Is this stage presence? Is this performative priestessing? Is this glamour magick? The answer is yes! Any individual who stands whole and fully holy in their authenticity and sovereignty possesses these same attributes, regardless of what they are wearing.

When we look at sacred connection and the act of sexual identification, we move beyond just the physical mechanics of bodies joining together. There is an immense difference in sex, fucking, making love, and being a sexual priestess. Knowing the differences, feeling each within your body, and understanding that as individuals we are the ones that dictate how each of these plays out in our inner and outer realms, we level up to a new kind of ownership and power.

In my brief stint with dating post-divorce, owning my sexuality and exuding it was not a chore or a have-to. It became a natural liberation. My body simply woke up! For me, it was a progression and elevation that took time – years of healing, releasing, and moving and sitting with myself on a personal level.

Let's face it; sex has been a very taboo topic! Yet we are bombarded with it everywhere, from music, movies, and books to billboards, posters and commercial ads. Sex sells! Why? We are all animals and sex is an instinctual urge, desire, and physical need.

How can one dive into and safely explore sex as a sacred connection? Not just with their partner(s) but with oneself first and foremost. Freya is the ultimate expression and example of sexual freedom.

In the book *Love, Sex, and Magick* by Sirona Knight, she writes, "You are the summation of your perceptions. Form follows thought, so your image of yourself forms your picture of reality. We are our images."

Before my divorce, I was wearing costumes that society approved of. I was a mother and a wife. But with divorce came the realization that my children were no longer children; they were adults in their twenties with lives of their own. My role of wife was dead, because I chose to kill that identification and discover who I really was outside of that role. It became a self-discovery that, while invigorating, also triggered those around me who were not accustomed to this me that was surfacing.

While I had embraced the outward expression of sacred adornment and I had moved through the death process of reclaiming my selkie skin, I now had to own and physically move into sex as a sacred connection.

When you connect with an individual for the first time, there is usually a level of timidness; insecurities surface with some self-doubts and inner questions. You can call it the awkwardness of dating.

While I didn't actively date, I was putting myself out in the public eye more and more. This consisted of going out, attending concerts, going to karaoke, and doing things I normally would not have done in the hopes of becoming more confident and gifting myself with the uncomfortableness of growth.

The other level of timidness naturally surfaces in the bedroom when clothing comes off and you are exposed with another individual that you have not connected with before. As humans, we have been taught to value other people's opinions, and, let's face it, body image is something that nearly every human being has struggled with.

Glamour magick, by Google's definition, is "a form of spiritual practice or magic that uses intention, visualization, and the power of aesthetics to enhance one's charisma, beauty, and confidence, or to influence how others perceive them. It involves imbuing items such as makeup, jewelry, or clothing with energetic intention to create a desired personal aura or shift the energy around oneself. The practice is rooted in the idea of using personal power to create subtle illusions or energetic transformations to manifest goals." Yes, Freya used glamour magick each time she wore Brisingamen.

Years ago, I traveled to Northern California to attend numerous goddess spirituality festivals, lectures, ceremonies, and conferences. Glamour magick was prevalent. The priestesses leading these events were dressed to impress! The amount of time and energy that went into creating their 'look' for each individual occurrence was impressive and a bit daunting.

This method of creation magick is highly effective, the intent being to captivate, ensnare, entice, and allure the bystanders to give all their attention to the one performing. This is performative work and we see it everywhere in this modern realm. There is nothing wrong with this method, as we all know it to be very effective. However, as individuals, we need to honor that this method should be unique to the individual and not a 'how-to' to recreate someone else's magick, but rather this method should be a way of inspiring individuals to create their own method, style, and intention.

When dressing to impress, or rather undressing, what is the intention? If you are taking time to connect with someone intimately, what is the intention? Who are you in the performance of your life? What is your stage, and who is acting with you?

> "All the world's a stage, and all the men and women merely players."
>
> William Shakespeare

Stripping down into the nude in front of a stranger can be very intimidating or uncomfortable, or it can be the opposite. It really depends on one's self-image.

> *"Sexual energy is one of the most potent energies in relationships. The ancients considered sexual intercourse sacred, providing an avenue to enlightenment and deity. Sexual activity and expression need to be seen as something empowering. When you make love, you create a vast amount of positive energy, and this can be used to promote the patterns and perceptions you desire. And it can be used to heal yourself, others, and the world."*
>
> Sirona Knight

To assist me with this liberation, my intent was to no longer hide my sexuality but display it in a form of glamour. If life is a stage and we are all actors, then sometimes we need to put on a show. More often than not, we need to stand up tall, dress to impress ourselves, and go out under the spotlights.

As human beings living in an ego-driven world, this can be scary. There are many ways, however, to overcome fears, and the best way is to just push through. What helped me the most was knowing that while I was uncomfortable and unsure, the chances are that the person I was connecting with was as well. Oftentimes this was expressed with body language and verbal cues.

If you are going to exchange energy in a very powerful manner, such as sacred sexual connection, one would hope that you take the time to communicate and engage before you get to the bedroom.

When I was invited over to my now husband's home for the first time, my intent was to engage in a casual connection. Our initial interaction was heavily anchored in an instant physical attraction with a very unexpected energetic and soulful activation.

Before I even arrived at his home, I gave myself a pep talk, and my friends gave me a pep talk because they knew my intention was to step into my prowess and bravery. I was reminding myself of my worth, my power, and my desire to reclaim my life as mine.

My intimidation factor stemmed from knowing that this man was the most attractive and confident man I had ever encountered. How he ended up in Utah of all places – at the time I was baffled. Before I even got out of my car, I asked myself, "What would Freya do?" This has become a catch-all phrase for just about everything in my life.

In my black tank top dress, I stepped out of my car, walked up his driveway, and entered, unbeknownst to me, my future. Our connection was intense from the first locking of eyes. This first night of sacred connection was mind-blowing. Not just physically but energetically, it was as if our bodies and souls had been searching for each other and had finally found one another.

My confidence was shaky; later I would learn that he was nervous as well. We were venturing into uncharted territory, at times in our lives when we were both healing from abusive relationships, and this connection was not on our radars. The universe is a tricky mistress, and when you finally get out of your own way, things tend to line up as they are meant to, whether you think you are ready or not.

In true gentleman style, I was given options – stay for another drink, sit and listen to some music, chat outside, or go to the bedroom. Since I was harnessing and welcoming Freya as my mirror, I chose the bedroom. Openly I will admit that my past was not filled with present lovers or even decent lovers. My sexual past was quite sad to reflect on, and like most women in their forties, it lacked the luster of bragging points.

This sacred connection, however, was otherworldly!

Being with an adequate lover, a present lover, and an incredible lover requires some skill and devotion to one's craft of sacred connection. It also requires equal participation. In my past, I was a possession, an object. My needs, wants, and desires were of no value.

Sex is one of those places where physical and spiritual love meet and become one. When you make love with intention, you oscillate collectively with your partner and become one large oscillator. Whenever you touch another person, an exchange of energy takes place between the two of you. Touch itself communicates energetic information and influences your personal energy field.

That first night we both had the same intentions, and that was to explore one another because we both felt an instant attraction and energetic connection. We both wanted to make the most of this night because we didn't think we would ever see each other again. So we did just that. We made the most of that night, and now we are married, and our sacred connection continues to rapidly expand each and every day.

> *"When you truly make love, you become the god and goddess, connecting with the sacred and merging with divine light. You recreate infinity and become the boundless."*
>
> Sirona Knight

Sexual rites and rituals have been practiced since the beginning of time. These are categorized by either culture-created or natural behavior. From fertility rites and rites of passage to blessing of the land to increase agricultural production and wedding ceremonies, these rites and rituals have been ongoing.

For example, May Day, May 1st or Beltane, is world-renowned for being heavily anchored into sex as a sacred ritual utilized to bless and increase the abundance of the land and community. Having myself attended the Beltane Festival held in Edinburgh, Scotland, I can express having witnessed first-hand the marriage of the May Queen to the Green Man and the passion and sensuality displayed during their ritualistic union.

Sexual priestess work, or sacred prostitution, is an ancient theme dating back to early Mesopotamia, Babylon, Egypt, and Greece. These women would engage in sexual rites as a way of transporting specific goddess energies to temples and their patrons. These were women-focused, women-empowered rituals designed to elevate the feminine and celebrate the body of creation, that being woman.

While sexual priestess work was deemed sacred and an act of worshipping goddesses, such as Aset (Isis), Inanna, Ishtar, and Aphrodite, to name a few, these ancient practices underwent attack when Christianity came to the forefront. As someone growing up in Utah, I observed this firsthand with the history retelling of Mary Magdalene. For those who know Mary Magdalene to be the bride of Christ and a priestess of Isis, the Church would later go on to describe her as a whore, a prostitute, and one who was a sinner, deemed unworthy and unclean.

In the book *The Magdalene Manuscript* by Judi Sion and Tom Kenyon, Mary describes herself as a 'priestess of ecstasy'. This concept of sex as a sacred connection was unfortunately demonized and frowned upon, especially by those who did not like Jesus having a wife. This act of

Jesus Christ as a husband and lover humanized him, which created an uproar.

Sex will always be a controversial topic. Sex workers will always experience support and hate. Those modern-day Heathens, Pagans, and witches that practice sex as sacred connection and openly speak on it will also receive positive and negative feedback.

I liken it to practicing skyclad. In my past, while attending goddess festivals that were women only, this act of standing naked in a ritual circle offended those who were not comfortable with their bodies and their own sexuality. In 2015, while offering my own Wild Women's Weekend with 33 guests in attendance, all women, I led a ritual skyclad as a way of mirroring to women that clothing creates a shroud that hides our ability to be full and whole within our bodies. There were two women present who were openly outraged and went so far as to call me a disgrace and shouted that I should be ashamed of myself and how dare I think I was fit to offer a women's empowerment weekend.

There are always going to be insecure people who object and express these objections loudly. Standing whole in one's sexuality and embracing one's body as something sacred should never be shunned. If you are uncomfortable, then that is where adult communication comes into play. No one is responsible for your triggers but you, the individual.

When it comes to sex as sacred connection, only you and your partner(s) can dictate the specifics. In this modern world, where we are being encouraged to express ourselves and openly identify our sexual preferences, we should not be regressing to close-minded thinking. Rather, let's continue to create spaces where we can celebrate our bodies and our ability to explore, play, and create ecstasy together.

## HOW TO MAKE THE MOST OF SACRED CONNECTIONS

- **Communication is VITAL!** If you are going to expose yourself physically and energetically to another individual, whether you are familiar with each other or not, communication must take place. As an individual, you need to express verbally what you want, what feels good, what doesn't feel good, what you are willing to try, and what you are not. Communication cannot be an afterthought. Communication needs to take place before your clothes come off!

- **Know your body!** Know your needs and know what feels good and what doesn't. This should happen long before you connect physically. This is an act of devotion that takes self-exploration. You should know your body inside and out. While doing yoga naked in front of a mirror helps one overcome negative body image, being comfortable with your own nudity in other facets also helps overcome body image issues and raises awareness of what your body looks like, feels like, needs, and desires. Nudity is normal! Or rather, it should be normal! After all, we are all naked under our clothes. We all possess skin that covers our bones. Get to know your curves, touch your body, and know your erogenous zones.

- **Explore your partner with curiosity and compassion.**
When you connect physically with another individual,
you are being given a new level of trust. Touch your
partner with curiosity and take your time to get to know
their body, their needs, and their desires. Pay attention
to how their body responds to different stimuli. Watch
their breathing; listen to their verbal expressions and
moaning. Sacred connection should be a form of play; it
should be exciting and powerful.

- **Avoid routines!** Connecting with a partner should not
be a chore, an obligation, or a routine. Spice things up!
If you are expected to engage sexually with your partner
or spouse on a day-to-day basis or on certain days, then
this connection can all-too-often become tainted and
resented. When sex is no longer exciting, there is a
problem! If you are required to engage in connection on
particular days, then the act itself is not welcome and
will not be a pleasant experience. Keep things new and
exciting!

- **Honor each other as kings, queens, gods, and
goddesses!** Whether your connection is committed or
casual, each time you lock up with another individual
physically, you are engaging in a deep and profound act
of sacred connection. Treat each other and each other's
bodies as that of royalty. When you do connect, know
that throughout history this physical engagement of two
becoming one was once considered and should always be
considered as HIGH MAGICK! Respect and honor should
take the forefront.

- **Be present as lovers!** In this world of hustle, bustle, and constant distractions, maintaining a level of presence in the bedroom can, unfortunately, be a challenge. Turn off the music, turn off your phones, and engage in sacred connection. Be fully engaged! Be fully present! Taking time to intentionally connect is similar to taking time to create ritual space. When you create ritual space, you prepare your body and soul to move into an act of intention. See, touch, and explore each other intentionally. Light candles, create a mood – or rather, a ritual space. Cast a circle of protection where distractions are not welcome.

- **Have fun!** Sacred connection should be enjoyable. It should be a form of play and exploration. If you trust each other, communicate with each other, and honor each other, then you should be able to have fun. Laughter during connection can be an amazing addition. Ecstasy explodes from the body in so many different ways. Be silly, be playful, and enjoy each other and the magick you are creating together.

## ACTIVATING SACRED CONNECTION AS A RITUAL

Those of you who actively practice your craft and engage in rituals and ceremonies will know that the ritual begins with setting the intention and preparing your ritual space.

Altar set-up, gathering supplies, and adorning oneself are all parts of the ritual. For this ritual, you will need to sit down with your partner and craft together your intention.

- **Intention is everything!** Make a date night, sit down and talk about your sex life. Are you both fulfilled? Do you want to try something new? What is it you are lacking or wanting more of? Make sure you communicate clearly, and, most importantly, listen without interrupting and shelve your ego. Heartfelt listening means listening. Really take time to hear each other without becoming defensive.

- **Create sacred space together:** Once you have set your intention, move into your ritual space and create the mood. Are you using candles? Maybe a circle of salt? Gather your ritual supplies. Create an altar together to help physically and energetically craft your intentions into the physical realm. Altars are, after all, mirrors of one's intentions.

- **Prepare your bodies for connection:** Physical stimulus is key in moving energy through your body and entangling it with your partner's. 'Kinesthetic touch' refers to learning or perceiving the world through the senses of touch and body movement, often combined in a hands-on, physical way to understand and retain information. Light-touch massage, soft kisses, and stroking each other are all ways to create this stimulus and activate kinesthetic touch. Be intentional with how you touch each other, and remember that you are both sacred and your union is sacred.

- **Move into connection as sacred ritual:** With your ritual space set, touch activated, and your intention vibrating within each of you, move into that sacred space of connection where two become one. Look at each other; devour each other with your eyes. Allow and maintain direct eye contact throughout. See each other – really see each other. Memorize each other. When you touch each other, see your hands exploring each other. Make sacred connection a visceral ritual.

- **Embrace the ecstasy afterglow:** Following your ritual, don't leave your sacred space right away. Take time to sip some wine, reflect, and communicate on which moments were your favorite. Continue to touch each other, hold each other, and see each other.

> *"Come together with your lover and drink the nectar of life, savoring every sweet droplet with succulent desire."*
> Sirona Knight

Sex as ritual should be focused on exploration, allowance, and enjoyment. We have been taught for far too long in society that sex is a dirty act and should be kept tucked away in the privacy of one's bedroom. This kind of close-minded thinking has unfortunately created shame, guilt, and rejection of one's body and passions.

We need to sit with each other's bodies, love every inch, and touch, taste, see, and feel. We need to make this sacred connection magick once more! We need to see our partner's body as uncharted territory, ready to be explored. Allow new sensations and pleasures to surface. Give each other permission to try new things and ultimately awaken the sexual prowess within each other.

Inviting Freya into one's sex life can be profoundly intense. On a personal level, I have never experienced such mind-blowing connections that often do not need to end with a physical mechanical release, as mine and my lover's connection is bound to exploration through unconditional love. We enjoy, savor, and ravage each other in so many ways outside of the bedroom that we are both completely satiated and ache for more … and more … and more …

# CHAPTER NINE

# Luscious Celebration

ᚠ

**B**asking in the afterglow of lusciousness is magick incarnate.

'Luscious' by definition means "having a delicious taste or smell." What if we as humans having a very human fuckery experience began to see moments, people, and life as luscious? Could we shift our perspectives enough to savor not just the good but also the bad?

As one who has been forced and bullied out of a home that my love and I were looking forward to staying in for the rest of our lives, this act of finding lusciousness seemed impossible! In fact, there were days when the stress was detrimental.

However, we as humans tend to limit our imagination, and we forget that each end-of-day result is not determined by one incident; it is determined by the overall experience – and, let's face it, each day we have on this planet is filled with innumerable moments, and most are not really all that terrible.

*"The imagination is precious. Don't lose it. Don't lose the child in you."*

Marilyn Manson

My king and I decided that if we were going to be bullied and forced to move from a home that he rightfully owned, we would go out with a bang and really celebrate. We planned the most gorgeous and intimate 'vampire wedding'. We spent the morning prepping our yard – the garden that we built, planted, and practically lived in – and we set up our wedding spot on our beloved wine platform.

We spent the rest of the morning and early afternoon lounging in our decadent yard, sitting in our bathrobes, sipping wine, and gazing into each other's eyes. There was no stress, no bride- or groomzillas. There were just two people so ready to fully and legally commit, embracing the lusciousness of our garden and our love.

We watched as a storm began to blow in, and we both smiled at the knowing that we were going to be blessed with rain on our wedding day. Rain is such a good omen – it washes away anything that no longer energetically serves the new couple, and we were ready for a cleansing.

As we prepared for our ceremony, changed into our clothes of dark red and black, and watched each other with hungry eyes and devotion, we knew that the ceremony would need to be moved from outside to inside, and we had already created that back-up plan.

As the guests arrived and my father, the officiant, helped us move the chairs, we were filled with bubbles of excitement – no nerves. The ceremony was intimate, short, and exactly what we both wanted. We had our wedding our way! We held hands, looked into each other's eyes, and expressed our unrehearsed and impromptu vows of committing to continue to love unconditionally.

After we fed each other cake, and celebrated with charcuterie and chatter, the guests left and we were alone. Candles lit, our song began to play, and we danced in our now empty living room as husband and wife.

Following our dance, we headed out into the now rain-blessed garden and began our fire ceremony. It was important that we welcome our guests to add written wishes, blessings, and add dried herbs, flowers, and spices to our first fire as husband and wife. With our goblets in our hands, the fire was lit, and we spent the rest of the evening until the early hours welcoming the glow of ignition into our future.

Living a luscious life can easily be obtained by stepping into the present moment. In this maddening society of hustle, bustle, and constant distractions, when you can be fully intuned to each magick moment, you can begin to truly savor the entirety of your life and all it has to offer.

Ritual magick is luscious magick in the flesh. When doing ritual, you create a space not within the mundane muggle world but contained within its own realm of protection and intention. What most people forget is that all of life is one big ritual. The challenge is finding the lusciousness in the despair and dark moments. Just a few nights ago, I was asked by my husband why I was so positive? We had both been consumed by the heaviness of emotional loss, the stress of moving, and the anxiety of thinking, "How do we move forward despite the current situation?" I had to pause and reflect on that before answering.

In reality, I am not a positive person. I am not a 'light and love' kind of witch, nor do I even like that metaphysical outlook. After sitting with it, my response was, "I love myself too much to allow myself to be devoured by the negative moments in my life." Again, we are humans having a very human experience, and shit happens! We live in a beautiful state that is, like any other state, filled with ugly people.

Moving forward means moving forward! Why stand in stagnant, mucky, putrid water and expect to stay clean and untainted? You have to move – physically, energetically, and spiritually. Movement is medicine.

Walking a labyrinth is meditation as movement. Most people struggle with the stereotypical meditation of deep breaths, with eyes closed, and silencing the chatter of one's inner mind. However, walking is meditation, and it can have profound effects. The art of walking in a pattern on the ground can be quite delicious as one's mind begins to shift perspectives and the body activates conscious presence with the act of moving.

My husband is an Aries, and he burns hot! I have no doubt that his fire, when activated (and which is always burning), could alienate those in his path who have wronged him. Here we were, experiencing three families in the neighborhood that intentionally wronged us as a couple and attacked him with legalities, as he was the homeowner. It is both inspiring and frightening to watch a wildfire, and his fire was ready to burn it all down. But that does not make him negative nor me positive. We just burn differently.

Music is meditation. When we first started dating, my music preference was eclectic but primarily consisted of Stevie Nicks, The Beatles, Manson, and 80s/90s rock. I had very little interaction with metal. My husband is a metal fan; it's his medicine, and me being an open-minded person, I will give anything a shot. So, he put on album after album, and soon our night turned into day as my body and soul awakened to a new magic.

As a literary person, words are my doorway to insight. While he played each song, I would read the lyrics, and we created a ritual of our own together that opened up our connection as a couple to so many powerful songs – songs that would mirror what we were experiencing on such profound levels, it was as if the artists wrote them for us.

## WATCH THE WORLD BURN – FALLING IN REVERSE

### written by Cody Quistad / Tyler Smyth

*"Yeah, I got voices in my head again.*
*Tread carefully and I don't medicate, it helps me temporarily.*
*I got problems, I got issues, yeah, apparently trauma that I'm*
*burying. I think I need some therapy.*
*I battle depression. I'm back with a message.*
*I'm asking the question that if you hate me,*
*why you acting obsessive?*
*I'm past the point of no return. Fuck being passive-aggressive,*
*I'll brandish a weapon, teach all you motherfuckers a lesson.*
*I actually battle my demons and shadows. They swim in the*

*deep, and they creep in the shallows. I'm lost.*
*I gotta admit that I'm living the life that I've always wanted,*
*but it comes at a cost.*
*They're licking their chops, they're fixing to rip me apart.*
*I'm swimming with sharks, I'm lifting the bar, I'm lifting it*
*into the stars.*
*I'm like a shot of adrenaline mixed with some Ritalin.*

*You started a battle, but bitch, I'ma finish it.*
*You think you can stop me? Not even a little bit.*
*Nowadays, everybody's so sensitive.*
*Taking my words and you pick it apart.*
*Tripping on nothing, just get in the car.*
*Gripping and ripping, I'm sticking the mark.*
*I'm tipping the ch-ch-ch-ch-ch-ch-charts.*

*'Cause I got enemies trying to get rid of me.*
*Evil tendencies are fucking with me mentally.*
*I got people that don't like me in the industry.*
*I can feel your energy, you are not a friend to me.*
*'Cause I have been to places that you never wanna go, yeah."*

*I got dirt on people, but they act like I don't know.*
*Yeah, I could do some damage, but I'll never rock the boat.*
*All it takes is one post, watch 'em fall like dominoes*

*You'll never get rid of me, too many mini-me's ripping my*
*imagery. You know my history, it ain't a mystery.*
*I put every enemy outta they misery.*
*Somebody, send me some positive energy.*

107

*About to go Darth, about to go Disney.*
*Into the darkness, into infinity and*
*shut you motherfuckers up, you listening?*

*Stacking every little pretty penny that I'm getting.*
*And I'm never giving in to anybody, always winning.*
*Never kidding when I die, I'm taking everybody with me.*
*You're never gonna get me, 'cause you'll never see it simply.*
*I'm a motherfucking god, you're a light yawn. I'm a time-*
*bomb, and the vibe's wrong, is this micon?*
*I'm killing the syllables with a loaded refillable. I'm a lyrical,*
*typical super villain, I'm venomous.*
*And I'm never gonna stop until they put me on top of the list. I*
*can't control the monster any longer that's inside.*

*The pain and sorrow left us hollow.*
*No tomorrow's hard to swallow.*
*Death is calling, so appalling.*
*Tightrope walking, now I'm falling down,*
*like missiles falling from the sky.*
*Come and save us.*
*The pain and sorrow left us hollow.*
*Here today, but gone tomorrow.*

*The pain inside is the fuel that drives.*
*This flesh and bone through blood-red skies.*
*The death defying, hypnotizing. One day you're gonna figure*
*out that everything they taught you was a lie.*
*Watch the world burn.*

*Ooh.*

*The fear is what keeps you alive.*
*Break the fucking chains, take back your life.*
*The fear is what keeps you insane*
*Break the fucking chains, take away the pain."*

## DEATHWISH – ARCHITECTS

written by Alex Dean / Dan Searle / Sam Carter / Tom Searle

*"There was a time for change,*
*I fear it came and went.*
*Who's gonna pick up the pieces?*
*Who will be left to repent?*
*The sun is burnt out black,*
*Now there's no turning back (hey, hey hey).*
*Now there's no turning back.*

*Yeah, I know you know,*
*that we've been living a lie.*
*Turn a blind eye,*
*until the day we die.*
*Maybe we've passed the point of no return.*
*Maybe we just want to watch the world burn.*
*We just want to watch the world burn.*
*Our collapse will be remission.*
*A planet scarred beyond all recognition.*
*Suicide in slow motion, is this the path that we've chosen?*
*Too cowardly to face this, we've got a fucking deathwish.*

*You want to play with fire?*
*Don't cry when you get burnt.*
*You gave us life, we gave back death in return.*
*The sun is burnt out black.*
*Now there's no turning back.*

*We will consume until there's nothing left.*
*Remember us as a waste of breath.*

*Yeah, I know you know,*
*that we've been living a lie.*
*Turn a blind eye, until*
*the day we die.*
*Maybe we've passed the point of no return.*
*Maybe we just want to watch the world burn.*
*We just want to watch the world burn.*

*I know you know that we've been living a lie.*
*Maybe we've passed the point of no return.*
*We just want to watch the world burn.*

*I want to believe that it all counts for something.*
*The writing is on the wall.*
*It's hard to accept that it was all for nothing.*
*All for nothing.*

*Yeah, I know you know,*
*that we've been living a lie.*
*Turn a blind eye, until the day we die.*

*Maybe we've passed the point of no return.*
*Maybe we just want to watch the world burn.*
*We just want to watch the world burn."*

To embrace and savor life, one simply needs to connect with each moment as delicious. We as humans need to taste both the sweet and the bitter. Music, movement, lovemaking, screaming, and crying are all ways to be fully consumed and present. I have always been a music lover, but until I met my king, I never tasted it.

To celebrate our wedding, we took a brief honeymoon to Las Vegas, which is only a couple hours from our new home. We chose to spend both nights at concerts. The first night we saw *In This Moment*, which was like witnessing a witches' ritual from start to finish. The theatrics are amazing and the music stirring. The second night we saw the one and only *Marilyn Manson* – an artist that was a must-see on both of our bucket lists.

He blew my mind! There were no theatrics, just an artist with no fucks to give who sang his heart out and fed the audience raw medicine.

My favorite moments were watching my husband smile and sing along and be one with the songs. He drank up that medicine and was swimming in lusciousness.

There are ample ways we can shift into a more consciously present way of living.

Taking time to connect with each other through active listening and heartfelt communication is one. Allowing each other to speak without response or reaction is huge! Music is a different form of communication, and when we can embody a song during hardships or joy, we can truly savor the conflicts and pleasures.

When you can combine music with a shift in perspective, you can sit upon your throne and look at things happening in your life with new eyes and ears. Combine that with a hunger for life, and all things are possible.

To taste life is to know that sometimes moments will be sour and sometimes they will be sweet. You can train your energetic taste buds, and that requires a desire to do so. One has to want change in order to manifest it. My husband is a master manifestor. Maybe it is his Aries fire? I have literally heard him speak something and then seen it happen, almost simultaneously.

Everyone is capable of manifesting a more luscious life, of living like royalty and being king and queen of their own castles, minds, and bodies. We can shapeshift our lives into something worthy of indulging in and savoring, and that is all through being present in all things.

When asked how I would describe my life, my answer has always been, "charmed." I live a charmed life. My existence is simple, but it's mine. Every aspect of my life has been like adding an ingredient to a large stew. I have chosen to add some spicy ingredients, some bitter ones, and some sweet and sour ones. But the choice has always been mine, so I cannot be positive or negative – it just is how I choose to see and taste it.

When my king and I anchor into our 'bubble', as we fondly call our stew of our brewing, we lose all track of time. We are so deeply invested in our connection that we indulge in the present moments. I have never felt a connection so deeply with another human being. This 'bubble' has become our safety. In each other's arms, we are home.

Freya shows presence and, as a battle queen, asks the big question: "What kind of luscious life are you willing to create and fight for?" How much can you shape your perspectives to see that life is beautiful chaos?

If all we truly have control over is each present moment, then we should dive into that and accept that we can ravage life. As kings and queens, let's taste life, savor it, roll it around on our tongues, and speak of just how luscious each day together can and will continue to be.

*"Embrace the chaos of now, for in its unpredictability, we find the beauty of living."*

Anonymous

# CHAPTER TEN

# Doorways of Insight

In my professional life, I am an author and a bookseller. I manage our local independent bookshop and love it on a level that no other job in my past could ever level up to. Books, like deities, have become friends, mirrors, and doorways into new ways of thinking, seeing, and being.

There are many doorways of insight that can help any individual transform, grow, and expand. After all, the definition of 'insight' is "the capacity to gain an accurate and deep intuitive understanding of a person or thing." Books were, during my marriage, an escape – a way to hide from any doorway that might liberate me, as I was honestly unsure of what I was willing and not willing to do.

The doorways in my post-divorce life that brought me the most insight were the ones that made me the most uncomfortable. Shadow work is something that modern-day practitioners discuss often. It is in the dark where we are forced to find our own light, to let the cracks illuminate truths that we fear and that our ego has taught us to resist.

Freya, if she was afraid of anything, didn't really show it. She was brave, tenacious, bold, and unwavering. She was a battle queen, a fierce lioness, a force whole unto herself. While she didn't exhibit fear on the outside, I am certain there were some apprehensions and insecurities that she felt but chose not to show.

Insight in the midst of being uncomfortable is truly seen mostly in hindsight, if I am being completely honest. We often look back in pride at how we handled something, while we second-guessed it at the time. Ego is a terrible human trait. One we all must grasp and handle, as we are not fortunate enough to be animals and be free of ego.

Insight comes in many forms: in the faces of strangers and from books, movies, and outlets that we normally take for granted. For me, in activating Freya, my greatest insight came from reflection on the battles I lost, fought, and would choose to never engage in again.

Google defines the 'doorways of insight' as "methods or perspectives that lead to deeper understanding or breakthroughs in various aspects of life, often related to personal growth, problem-solving, or spiritual development. These can be practices, concepts, or even physical spaces that act as catalysts for change or revelation."

## PHYSICAL SPACES

Every queen needs her own castle, her own space, her own sanctuary. Hindsight was and is one of life's greatest teachers.

In the middle of December, a pipe froze underneath my newly renovated bathroom, and I was sitting barefoot on the coldest night of the year, doing my best to find the freeze and unfreeze it. Alone, under my house of 22 years, anger and frustration were the only things keeping me warm. It was in this anger that I knew in every fiber of my being that I could no longer be anchored into this physical space.

It was no longer my home or my castle. The very next day, I sought a new perspective and pulled out a ladder from the shed and climbed up on top of the roof. Gazing out at the landscape of my yard that I had tended every inch of for over two decades, I felt a huge disconnect.

As queens, we must often take inventory of what is serving our inner growth and what is no longer serving our inner growth. This home, this life, was no longer serving me. So, I made the decision to sell the house and split the cost with my ex. While in the beginning he was in agreement, it soon became evident that ulterior motives were taking the forefront. No paperwork was signed, only an offer to buy me out.

Queens of sovereign self are open to receive counsel. After all, I had welcomed in Freya; now came the question, "Was I willing to listen to her counsel?" After many tears, staring down quite literally my past that I had crafted out of a need for security came the answer that I had been resisting for 13+ years. This castle and what it once stood for was only a temporary resting place, and it was time to move on.

Blood money was accepted, boxes filled, and a major purge took place. My beloved goddess temple that had held countless ceremonies over the past eight years was closed, statues were put into storage, and a bonfire was lit. Quite literally, as queen, I was burning my past. Now the building sits – an empty a home with blacked-out widows. One major book of my life closed.

My lover opened up his home, his castle, and with that, a new chapter in my book of life opened, ready to be written. Physical spaces are doorways; they teach us so much about security. What does it feel like when one is actually safe and secure, and what does it feel like when one is not? This was a space that I had built, loved, and cared for, and I was more than willing to walk away from it only because I had learned that some battles were no longer worth the fight. If I had stayed, I would have been tethered to old memories, my past, and projects that were never completed that I would have had to complete. With my head held high, I said goodbye and welcomed the insight that no physical space would determine my worth.

Another major doorway was to craft and create new **practices.** As humans, we thrive on routine and the familiar structure. In my old life, my day would begin with structure. 20 minutes of yoga, breathwork, and a cold shower. After six years of doing yoga on a twice-a-day routine, never skipping a single day, one of the greatest doorways of insight (that shocked just about everyone that knew me) was that I stopped.

My mornings began slowly, entangled up in bed with my lover. We welcomed the days with kisses, tender words, and Baileys-infused coffee or a thick breakfast stout. No longer did I feel the need to literally twist my body and shape it into a form that others would find desirable or approve of. My body became my own.

Releasing 50 pounds of inflammation that was creating a false security created liberation and a self-love that was totally new and invigorating. Happiness seeped out of every pore of my body, and where yoga was once a celebration of my body, being able to move with fluidity and grace, celebration came from loving my body as it was.

Can you imagine Freya going to the gym every day, running five miles, lifting weights, or doing yoga twice a day? Neither could I. Freya was whole unto herself as her full self. Her body was her temple; it was neither perfect nor imperfect. It was simply hers. That knowing in itself made her desirable. She could share it with others, or not.

My body became my own. My new practice was to live fully present within my body and physical space as queen. Ditching old practices was liberating! Moving out and away from the routines and living moment-to-moment was exhilarating!

There was no set bedtime or morning alarm clock. There was the occasional adulting, like going to work or going to the store for groceries. But the once-set practice of living, structured hour-by-hour, was no longer a priority. This act of rebellion against the norm was a very powerful insight. It was in this act that I found the true essence of magick, and that was living present in the moment.

The concept of 'working to live' took the forefront and became a new doorway of insight. During my 24-year marriage, I was living with someone who was hyper-focused on living to work. With hindsight, this was his way of creating security and also escaping a toxic relationship and home life. My ex lived to work – he worked simply to make money.

My lover worked to live. Not for monetary gain like my ex did, but because it kept his mind busy. This concept of working to live would become not just a doorway of insight for me but also for my new love.

Money is something that I was blessed to not have a relationship with; maybe it was because I never had it. But money was something you earned to put food on the table. I never had any idea of savings, 401(k), or retirement funds. If I needed money for groceries, I would ask for some, or I would sell some books or herbal tea blends. Money was something used to get by, not acquire and have.

Recently obtaining blood money for my temple and my share of what the house was worth was foreign to me; not to mention that I was shorted about $50,000, but again, I made the decision to walk away, so I was not going to complain. What I was going to do was take that blood money and do something for me and my new life.

As a queen, I took matters into my own hands, and with my king, we purchased a 'chariot' together – or rather, a 2013 Mercedes-Benz Sprinter van, fully hooked up with a bathroom, bed, and kitchen and dining area. We hit the open road.

Together, we gave up the concept of living to work and embraced working to live. We took our two Corgi puppies with us and spent more time in the RV than we did in our home. We ventured out into nature, eager to disconnect from the riffraff, and found solace in nature. Money is there, and if we need more, then we take jobs and make more.

Being stagnant and tied down to a building, even if we love our home, which we do, was no longer going to be the only absolute. The concept of living within the safe confines of what society encourages in order to be a respectable participant in the human race was no longer fulfilling.

Being fully present in the rat race of society was and still is the most pleasurable doorway of insight. While on a two-week cross-country road trip, we allowed ourselves to be fully present, fully engaged – and with that came complete healing, love, and bliss.

There were ample nights when we would stay up sitting by our campfire, just talking about anything and everything until the sun rose. In my heart of hearts, I imagine Freya doing something similar with her warriors, ladies, and many loves.

Something in society broke with the creation of cell phones and social media. We as humans stopped interacting and connecting with each other. Texting took the place of phone calls. Phone calls took the place of letters. Letters took the place of traveling to actually visit a loved one face-to-face.

Modern technology, with all its advantages, has some very clear disadvantages.

Covid broke society in a new way, especially in the United States. Engaging in real conversation that consists of eye contact and active listening has become such a rare concept that now when someone makes eye contact or actually listens without interjecting, it is viewed as aggression or confrontational.

Life on the road is not without its challenges and hooking-up stresses. There are a lot of things to learn about a house on wheels that are drastically different from a stationary home. However, the most profound lesson was that neither our stationary house nor our house on wheels was actually *home*.

Another major concept that would be a doorway to insight was that a house is quite literally walls with a ceiling and floor. A home is a completely different entity and vibe alltogether. Much like a castle that is stone and mortar, the energy comes from the people who lived within, who gave it warmth and life. My home would become a person.

Homes are built upon concepts, this general notion or abstract idea. Is your home a place, a notion, or a concept? My previous home was a place tethered to the idea that if I decorated it to reflect me and my wants, it would become a notion for security.

My present home holds the new energy of two people who want liberation from old relationships, and it is filled with the emotions of love, refuge, and peace. Our home on wheels is much the same, only it comes with the momentum that we are king and queen, so we can and will take this home wherever we want to go and enjoy every moment – in reality, all our physical spaces that hold and carry the energy that we, the inhabitants, install within it.

Home as a person is the ultimate insightful discovery. This person who I met thanks to universal timing has become all of the things a tangible physical space should have been. Within his acceptance of me as my own person, his arms have become the security of walls, ceiling, and floor. He has become my home, and I have never felt so safe, seen, appreciated, adored, cared for, and loved.

In order to really expand as individuals, we have to be willing to open the doorways of insight – even if they are scary. Take the risks, put yourself out there, shelve the routines, and push back against what society wants you to believe you are supposed to be doing. This is, after all, your one big life – so, live it loudly, live it BIG!!!

## WAYS TO ACTIVATE THE DOORWAYS OF INSIGHT

Routines create structure – which creates a false sense of security. You are not any more safe than you were yesterday; you are just comfortable in your complacency and self-established routine.

Do something different every day! Get up on the opposite side of the bed, brush your teeth using your other hand, skip the gym, call in sick, and take yourself out for coffee, wear something you have always wanted to but were too focused on other people's opinions to actually wear it, take yourself out to lunch, arrange a meet-up with an old friend.

Do something different every day!!! Break your own patterns, flip off the routine, and swim against the current.

Concepts are meant to be broken. After all, the definition of 'concept' is "an abstract idea or general notion." Be abstract! Create your own rules and definitions. Say goodbye to what society says is normal, how a relationship should look, or what roles each person should be fulfilling in a relationship. Be abstract! Push back against society and be bold, be true, be you. Better yet, be undefinable!

Just be you! Stop putting yourself into boxes. Ditch the labels.

With social media came hashtags, pronouns, and labels used to express who you are to those on the outside looking in. Who cares? What if you just got out of bed each day and decided to live your life to the fullest for you without having to identify yourself to or explain your actions to others? Just be you!

No explanation, no titles, no definitions, no cares or fucks about what other people think – just be you!

Practices are created. We as humans develop day-to-day practices and routines. These practices often pertain to ideas, beliefs, and methods that we were taught by our parents, teachers, or peers.

Create your own practice. Do you! Combine the doing of something different every day with the being you, and live your life by your own set of rules. Be your own source of insight and open up all the doorways that the universe is offering you. Most of the time, we are stuck on autopilot, and we don't even realize that the universe is one big cookie shop, just waiting for us to actually place our order of what kind of cookie we want to eat. Create your own practice for you, because you are worthy of whatever kind of magnificent cookie you want to devour.

If insight is defined as "the capacity to gain an accurate and deep intuitive understanding of a person or thing," then shouldn't we as individuals strive to obtain a deeper intuitive understanding of ourselves?

What are the doorways that you want to open up for yourself? How intuitively do you actually know and, more importantly, love yourself? How much time do you actually spend with yourself, as yourself? We as humans get so lost in making efforts to change ourselves for others that we ultimately lose touch with who we really are. In actuality, we are already whole and holy – let's start living like we are!

Yes, I understand that this sounds simple – and it is and it really isn't. One has to 'deprogram' oneself; and that does take time, dedication, and commitment. There are going to be days where you wake up and feel the complete opposite of royalty. Some days are going to be better than others, but the key is in making the most of each moment that you consciously can – and you can consciously choose to do just that.

Surround yourself with people who know you as you, and love you unconditionally. When you set a goal, let these people know so that they offer you encouragement on those not-so-great days and moments where you doubt yourself.

(see https://www.cocotique.com/blogs/blog/the-key-to-living-a-luscious-life)

# CHAPTER ELEVEN

# Ritual of Activation

"Repetition brings conviction."

This one line is the only thing I remember from Sunday school. I believe I was aged fourteen, and my teacher said this line over and over again for about three minutes. Now here I sit, some 32 years later, and I can still hear his voice and see the look on everyone else's faces as he sat in front of a group of early teens and repeated over and over again, "Repetition brings conviction … Repetition brings conviction …"

We have all heard that practice makes perfect, but who wants perfection if we are focused on accepting just how gloriously fucked-up we all really are as imperfect individuals? The key word is 'practice'.

Much like repetition, the more you do something physically and express something vocally, the more your physical body and mind remember it, and you create in your body a muscle memory – a knowing that, even if your eyes are closed, you could still see yourself moving through the motions of.

When it comes to ritual, we create an energetic activation of one's intention into the physical. This starts with intention.

Recently, I sat in on a circle of business owners, all wanting to create a community free of competition, comparison, and capitalism. I was invited to help jump-start things, and I began with one question: "What is your intention?"

Birthing a Pagan/Heathen/Wiccan community/coven/grove takes some time, energy, and serious planning if you are going to make it thrive. Intention sets the tone.

Just like when you wake up each day – what is your intention for that particular day? A goal, an idea, a dream, a desire, or a must-get-done list never hurts and helps you stay focused on the priority of that intention, rather than being bombarded and consumed with monkey brain.

As priestess in what can feel like a performative setting, one must be pre-prepared with not just intention but also the tools necessary to physically create an aesthetic presentation and experience for those in attendance.

When I first started offering group rituals, my planning began months in advance with the setting of a date and time and then the intention basis for each ritual. This foundational planning helped me to stay centered and get prepared and allowed those who were helping me to assist more efficiently.

When it comes to preparing your ritual of activation with Freya, what is your intention? Which aspect or attribute of Freya's are you wanting to invoke and call upon? Are you ready to welcome in more passion into your current relationship? Are you wanting to welcome in a new relationship? Are you wanting to heal your relationship with yourself? Are you wanting to ignite and invite more abundance? Are you ready to see yourself in the mirror of royalty and sit upon your throne? Are you ready to turn your home into a castle?

Sit with your thoughts, sit with your insecurities, and look into the mirror. First things first – set your intention.

While there is no right or wrong way to create a ritual of activation, there are some excellent tips available. While you have set your intention, it is a good idea to also plan a day or evening for your ritual. Are you doing your ritual in tune with a particular moon phase? If so, then do some research. Take the time to plan ahead!

Full moon magick is perfect when you want to illuminate things in your life.

After all, that is what the full moon does – it illuminates! Full moon magick is my favorite time for setting big intentions, to see the abundance in full swing in my life, and to quite literally shine down on all the good in my life.

New moon magick works great for releasing, healing, and going deep into the dark of one's psyche to pull out and tend to those things kept hidden. The new moon for me is the time to let the deep darkies within surface. Of course, these are my opinions, and one should formulate one's own working relationship with each moon cycle.

*"Your magick is your magick, and it should be defined, crafted, and practiced often by you for you."*

Friday is a popular day to call upon and work with Freya. The word 'Friday' stems from Old English, meaning 'Day of Frigg'. While many would argue that Frigg is her own unique deity from Norse mythology, others will argue that Frigg and Freya are one and the same. Again, you decide.

Friday's are the end of most people's working week, and there is an inner and outer celebration that happens when one gets to the weekend. To combine Freya's energy with Friday just seems fitting in, again, my opinion. Freya is all about liberation, celebration, and stepping into one's freedom. Freya's day is Friday! After a long working week, there seems to be an energetic shift when Friday arrives – like a breath of fresh air! Friday is a liberation day, a break from the grind of work, and an invitation to let loose and enjoy the weekend, to make plans and go out and about!

Friday the 13th is another excellent day to create a ritual of activation for Freya.

While, yes, there are many superstitions surrounding Friday the 13th (and Hollywood did a great job in making this date infamous for murder and mayhem, thanks to Jason, the man in the hockey mask), this particular date is numerologically a day for inviting good luck and abundance, at least for most witches who have chosen to ignore the superstitions behind it. Admittedly, I was confused why the number thirteen had such a bad reputation, so I indulged in my own rabbit hole of research and learned that this number is connected to none other than Loki (who I adore), as he was the thirteenth guest. Judas, who betrayed Jesus, was also the thirteenth guest at the Last Supper.

It is interesting where superstitions comes from, but again, the more you repeat and believe something, the more convicted your beliefs become.

Friday was also the day that Jesus was crucified, so not everyone loves Friday or the number 13. I will adopt the mindset that any day can be a lucky day, but Friday the 13th is one that the popular magickal community can agree upon as Freya's day!

Why is it lucky? For those of us who cycle each month, as the feminine, the number 13 is potent! We have thirteen cycles each year. There are also thirteen moon cycles each year. The number thirteen is connected naturally to the feminine, birth, creation, fertility, and energy to manifest! Most traditional covens have twelve members and a leader, or high priestess, giving life to the number thirteen, and you could say that's another reason for those non-magical folk to dislike it.

Friday the 13th is the day of goddess energy. As I have explained in my previous books, goddess is all-encompassing. When you break the word up, you get 'god' and 'dess' – a blending and balance of masculine and feminine. This day is particularly in sync with Freya, and it is fitting to activate a ritual that harnesses and honors all of Freya's feminine prowess, beauty, and pizzazz!

Years ago, while hosting a Wild Wolf Women's weekend, the entire three days and three nights were anchored into big feminine magick. We ended the weekend on Friday the 13th with a ritual dedicated to none other than Freya! There were thirteen women dressed in black with their conical hats on, circling under the full moon, and it was one of the most glorious rituals I have ever had the privilege of participating in.

Spontaneous ritual can be done on a whim when the mood strikes and is often the most powerful. However, for this chapter, the focus is on creating a practice to help one birth one's intentional craft. So, always trust your gut and do you!

With your intention set and date set, now comes the fun aesthetic part, and that is gathering up all your supplies if you choose. For me, simplicity is key, but I have attended the most elaborate rituals, and the visceral visuals were not just a bonus; they were almost more stimulating than the person(s) leading the ritual.

Elaboration is an art! Adding these visual details sets the tone immediately.

Over one year ago, about six months after the finalization of my divorce and numerous dates later, I went out into my goddess temple and set up the most elaborate and decadent altar to Freya. The round table was draped in crushed vermillion velvet and scattered with fresh blood-red rose petals. In the center was a statue of Freya. Next to her was a statue of Medusa, and on the other side a statue of Aphrodite. Three powerhouse deities! On gold star-shaped mirrors, I placed tea light candles, and on each side of Freya, two large red tapered candles were lit.

Red is a visceral and stimulating color! Red represents passion, sex, femininity, blood, death, and rebirth. It also is a color used to represent fire. Freya rituals naturally ignite a fire of passion within. Think candles, heat, and flame! Lots and lots of candles!!!

Rose petals are also associated with sex and passion. While any variety of rose will do as an offering of dedication to Freya, red is, of course, my personal favorite.

Dark chocolate and red wine are excellent libations to offer to Freya on the altar and to consume, as they are both luscious and invite that decadent Freya essence.

Ritual is a form of expression – a physical way of setting intention in motion. It can be compared to worship, but again, that all depends on the individual. For me, ritual is my way of physically crafting what it is I want. The more you move through ritual, the more you shapeshift your reality into what you really want. It's the conviction of creation. It's the Abracadabra – I speak therefore I create!

Each day should be a ritual. There should be an intention set, sacred adornment, libations, and movement to activate one's intention into creation. If we as humans took time to create each day consciously, then we would enjoy more luscious and decadent lives.

When I called upon Freya one year ago, it was to set into motion my life as a liberated divorced woman! While my single life was short-lived, I was and still am that liberated woman that stood naked and exposed. My ritual of activation was my self-adoration – a self-love ritual. It was a promise made to Freya with her as a mirror of my full potential to never give up on myself, water myself down, or compromise myself for anyone ever again!

131

Standing in front of the altar, I adorned myself with body oil that I had charged under the previous full moon. Oil infused with rose petals and frankincense. With the candles lit, I caressed, explored, and touched my body with rose petals as if they were the fingers of a lover. I sang songs, whispered hopes and dreams, and sat with my longing to find a king that was worthy to rule beside me.

My intentions were all over the place, but at the same time they were focused on me, just me the individual, crafting the life and love that I have always dreamt of and deserved. Conversations, tears, and heartfelt purging were cried out as I knelt in front of the altar. It was this ritual of activation that prompted me to channel Freya and write this book and to shelve the chaos of Loki that had been the catalyst for my divorce – and it would be Freya that would soften my hate and my malice and give me space to blossom.

Every book becomes a memoir! There is a piece of each author that can only come out onto the pages in written form. For me, this book is not just a memoir but also a love story. What began as a rejection of titles, societal roles, and the stigmas of being a wife has been transformed – healed through love by a love unexpected.

Freya taught me to believe in love again – the kind of love that as a child and young adult you only see in movies, make-believe, and romance novels. Freya brought me a sailor, a king, a best friend, the ultimate paddle boat companion, a soulmate, and a twin flame, and every day he reminds me that I am beautiful exactly how I am. Every day he encourages me to rise up and be the queen that I was born to be, because every day he sees me as such.

Freya, like Loki, is a catalyst! A shapeshifter! A queen! A goddess supreme! She is a mover, a shaker, and a magick-maker. She will challenge you, invigorate you, inspire you, and at times piss you off! Like any true motivator, she will, if you allow her to, surface as a mirror and rock your fucking world!

Freya is THE liberation of a Friday after a long, tumultuous working week. She is the strong drink that warms you on the coldest of nights. She is the flame that burns within you, offering you energy to keep going, and keep doing, and she reminds you to never give up on your hopes and dreams. Move through ritual dedicated to Freya, and she will activate you on every level.

Repeat your ritual as often as needed until you manifest your intention!

*"It's the repetition of affirmations that leads to belief, and once that belief becomes a deep conviction, things begin to happen!"*

Muhammad Ali

# CHAPTER TWELVE

# All Hail the Queen!

Freya is queen – not just of the Valkyries, but she is also queen of her sovereign self!

She is ruler supreme of her body and sexuality. She stands alone as the epitome of independence, confidence, assertiveness, and as goddess!

As any single individual will tell you, what they seek and what they long for in their single life is freedom. This freedom, while defined by the individual self, typically stems from a place of being controlled, stifled, muzzled, and bound.

Freya holds firm in her ability to create boundaries that will not allow others to interfere with her right to stand whole and holy as her full self – boundaries being key to any queen or king when ruling their kingdom. After all, can you imagine Freya bound, tethered, chained, or held against her will? NO!

As I maneuvered through what at first was an amicable divorce, which quickly became hostile, holding onto my boundaries was my salvation. No longer was I willing to compromise who I was, fear who I was with, and bow down to anyone other than myself.

A queen, after all, stands supreme and knows her worth! This is non-negotiable!

For far too long, I had made myself small, doused my flame, and hid who I was. The best way to assert boundaries is to write them down, read them, memorize them, and never be afraid to assert them!

While fully embracing the dating world and exploring the possibilities of connections, not just with romantic partners but with hopeful friends, it was vital that my boundaries were clear. This was made simple with a bit of self-reflection and contemplation. I took my journal out, grabbed my pen, and began to really sit with my past queendom to see what I no longer wanted and look with hope to what kind of queendom I was willing and ready to welcome in. My questions looked like the following (question, then detailed response):

* **What kind of friends do I want?**
- Friends that see me as me, help me to laugh, celebrate my authenticity, and allow me space to ride the waves of my chaotic life.

* **What activities do I want to do with these friends?**
- Dance parties, bonfires, hiking, adventures outdoors in nature, dinners, movies, and late-night chats.

* **What kind of lover do I want?**
- A lover who is selfless, wants to savor the experience, enjoys giving and receiving pleasure, communicates clearly, respects, is whole within their body, knows how to kiss, and understands that sex and intimacy are very distinct and powerful.

* **What kind of king do I want and deserve?**
- One who communicates, one who is brave and confident, knows their self-worth, and stands supreme in their boundaries, wants, and desires. Someone I can rule beside, not behind or beneath.

* **What does my castle look like?**
- My castle reflects who I am; it is filled with things that bring me joy and adorned with my favorite colors, a safe space where I can relax, heal, and be just me.

As rulers of our life (after all, if this is our one big life, shouldn't we be determined to live it to its fullest?), as individuals, creators, and gods/goddesses of our day-to-day life, we have the one and ONLY right to establish parameters that celebrate the life we are choosing to create!

Be specific with the universe, and most importantly, be specific with yourself.

Knowing your worth is one thing; demanding that others see and respect your worth can be a battlefield!

As queen, Freya is one who is known to ride into battle on her chariot pulled by large cats. She is Queen of the Valkyries – female warriors who ride into the battlefield and

137

hand-pick the fallen warriors who have earned the right to sit beside Odin in the Hall of Valhalla. Freya, as queen, has the final say! She can overrule the Valkyries' judgment.

As queens and kings of our kingdoms, we TOO have the final say over who is allowed to sit at our table and visit our queendom/kingdom. Do we exert this power? Or do we fall into the social norm of compromising our boundaries because we do not wish to offend anyone or hurt someone's feelings, or because we are second-guessing our right to actually assert these kinds of boundaries?

In our modern world, where everyone and everything is offensive, is it really offensive to demand respect in our own personal space? Or is it essential? Freya, in my experience, is not a soft, gentle deity. She is firm, assertive, and queenly!

When we sit with our boundaries, we should also take time to sit with our own definitions. What does being a queen or king mean to you as an individual? We can look to the dictionary to see the definitions offered, but then one needs to really sit and apply those definitions to their own experience, life, and realm.

> 'Queen' is defined as "the female ruler of an independent state." To be 'queenly' is defined as: "dignified, behaving in a way as if she is very important."

> 'King' is defined as "the male ruler of an independent state." To be 'kingly' is defined as "having royal rank within one's kingdom."

Regardless of what gender you anchor into, as individuals we are ALL rulers of our own unique independent states.

We each possess the capability to stand dignified, confident, supreme, whole, and holy, and establish our rank within our inner and outer realms of this life!

While most agree with this, what they lack is the actual gumption to stand up and exert the assertiveness to ensure that these boundaries are respected. As humans, we compromise more than we should. We second-guess ourselves, and we doubt ourselves. We cower, bow down, and think our assertiveness is aggressiveness – and because of this, we don't follow through.

Aggressive behavior is deemed offensive. Or is it assertive? Where is our accountability as individuals and our ownership? If someone is repeatedly told that their behavior is aggressive, isn't it only natural that they begin to label and believe themselves to be aggressive? What if someone simply told them that their behavior was assertive?

As queens and kings of our sovereign selves, we must also own that our perception of how we view others, view ourselves, and allow ourselves to be viewed is really and truly up to us. NO ONE can formulate an opinion on us unless we give them permission to do so.

Throughout my divorce, there were, unfortunately, many opinions directed at me. Most were unsolicited, and almost entirely none of them necessary. Why is it that as humans we feel we have the right to project our personally formulated opinions of others onto other individuals?

My motto has been, "Happy is a vibe!" Before my divorce, I was unhappy, borderline depressed, nearly obese, and miserable. When I finally filed and signed papers, I stood in my realm as queen, and I invited, created, and moved into a state of happiness that oddly pissed people off.

My message box was bombarded with people who had been merely observers in my life, reaching out to let me know that my happiness was offensive, fake, a smear tactic, and malicious. It was wild! When we look back at history and we see queens and kings happy, ruling their countries, and thriving, it makes you wonder how many times they were attacked for their ability to rule and maintain their unique happiness.

Freya is not one who cowers, bows down, second-guesses herself, or even dares to care what others think of her. She stands supreme! The quest of life has become to live life authentically empowered as our full selves in a fake world.

Can we embody Freya in this quest? Can we stand as individuals of our queendoms/kingdoms and demand respect? Can we stand before our lovers, friends, co-workers, and acquaintances and hold firm in our knowing that we are whole and holy, regardless of whether we are in the bedroom, at work, in the grocery store, or in our own homes? Can we rise up? Can we level up?

## ALL HAIL THE QUEEN MEDITATION ACTIVATION

*Settle into a comfortable position, free from interruptions. Bring your focus and awareness to your breath and take a nice deep inhale, followed by a long exhale. Breathe in to the count of four, and out to the count of four. With each breath, give your physical body conscious permission to relax, releasing all* tension as your subconscious moves deeper into the realm of possibilities fueled by your imagination.

Once in this state of physical and mental relaxation, you are ready to journey deeper. See yourself in your mind's eye, sitting upon a throne. This is your throne; it can be as simple or as elaborate as you wish to envision it. Take a few deep breaths and really create in your mind a throne that reflects who you are – who you really are.

When you see yourself sitting upon this throne, begin to shift your focus onto what you are wearing. What adornment, which style of clothing depicts you as your whole self?

Really see yourself on your throne, dressed as the royal being that you are.

Now look outward into the realm of your queendom/kingdom. Who is invited into your castle? Who has earned the right to see you as your whole self? Who respects the throne of authenticity that you and all individuals have the right to claim? Who is welcomed, by you, for you, into this space? Really see them – see their faces, hear their cheers of celebrations, see their adoration.

As you appreciate these people in your life that are sincere and value you as sovereign being, who stand before you in your realm, you begin to hear taunting jests in the background. These ugly sounds, shouts, and snide comments are coming from people in your life that are not interested in honoring your boundaries, people in your life that do not see you through eyes of respect. These are people who repeatedly have shown you disrespect and malice.

These people are no longer welcome! See yourself standing up from your throne. See your crowd of supporters pause in *silence as they watch you. The room before you parts, and you see two groups of people – those who are in support, and those who are not. It is time to clear your realm.*

*Standing tall, poised, and confident, you simply state, "Those of you who do not see me as the supreme, sovereign being of my own authenticity will leave, right now! I no longer will allow you to take up space in my realm. I no longer will permit you to disrespect my boundaries. You will leave right now!" See as, one by one, these individuals excuse themselves, turning their backs and walking away, never to be seen again.*

*As the final person leaves, an eruption of cheering comes from your crowd of supporters, your friends, your co-workers, your lover, your people! The ones that have stood by you through thick and thin. These individuals have never asked you to compromise who you are; they have only celebrated your strengths, loved you through your hard times, and walked beside you, as they too are kings and queens of their own realms.*

*You sit down upon your throne once more, your castle clear and your fans cheering loudly, "All hail the queen!" "All hail the queen!" "All hail the queen!" Breathe that celebration energy into your physical body. Let the joy, love, and allowance permeate your entire body. Soak it up! You have earned the right to be surrounded by people who love you unconditionally and see you whole and holy as your full self.*

Moving through meditation is an activation. The best way to follow through is to really embody all aspects of your life as queens and kings. Make a list of the people in your life that see you, love you, respect you, and truly want the best for you. Then make a list of the people in your life that seem to only want to be in your life out of some kind of ulterior motive.

Once you have your two lists, then the work of being a queen begins. After all, Freya does not allow just anyone to sit at her table or feast in the Hall of Valhalla, and neither should you. It is more than okay to excuse people in your life that drain you of your life. People who are constantly dragging you down and causing you to question yourself as a powerful being do not deserve to take up space in your 'bubble' of life.

This is a hard boundary, and ego will come into play. Rise up and rule over your castle – after all, you are the only one that can. Divorce is messy; not always but typically. One thing I learned was that not everyone who was my friend would remain a friend. Most mutual friends chose to pick sides in a marriage they were never married into. Sad, but true.

Stepping into the queen I deserved to fully embody meant that many would be excused from my life. This started with my ex, his family, most friends acquired during our marriage, and many acquaintances who thought they had the right to formulate and assert opinions on something that I should have done a decade ago.

Being royal in one's life also means taking ownership of one's castle. Take back your throne and pick and choose who comes into your physical space. Once papers were signed, I took my castle back! I gutted my bathroom, tore out the shower and corner tub, repainted, hung new light fixtures, installed new faucets, and finally installed the antique clawfoot tub that I had always wanted. If my bathroom was where I was most vulnerable, able to shed, clean, and rebirth, then I was determined to make my bathroom fit for the queen I have always been.

When I sat with Freya in meditation, with my candle lit, and asked for her strength, the one thing I heard and felt in response to my pleading was, "Rise up and be the queen of your life." These might sound like simple words, but following through is hard, and in life every choice has consequences. In my quest to create my castle for me and live my life for me, there were many people wounded on my battlefield of life. Or were there…?

Looking back at my queen rise up, I have zero regrets. Those people in my life that were excused played their part and were ultimately responsible for their excusal. As queen, I played my part too, and in my past there were many times that I did not level up – I did not see and love me as my truly fucked-up, glorious self. Looking forward, I will never tolerate less than I deserve or less than I give.

One thing that I was called often throughout my divorce and the months that followed was 'selfish'. This was odd to me. Aren't we as individuals entitled to be selfish and live our lives to the best of our individual needs? Was I *lacking consideration for others* by choosing to put my happiness first? Shouldn't we as humans on some level focus on our own personal pleasure?

When did society collapse our common sense? Why has it become more socially acceptable for people to stay where they are not welcome, loved, or appreciated, rather than to leave that realm of toxicity? Why are people who rise up and reclaim their rights to be safe, loved, and happy crucified and condemned?

As queen and as a human in this ego world, I have come to embrace that no matter what I do in my life, I will be a villain to some and a hero to others. But those outside opinions have no power over me. As a queen, like Freya, I rule my inner realm and my castle alone, and in my aloneness I have found a strength unwavering.

*"Alone, by herself, she built the kingdom that she wanted."*
R.H. Sin

What does it feel like to be queen of self and one's life? Liberating! If I wer to be perfectly honest, I would say there are times where loneliness surfaces. When this happens, I think of those ancient queens, alone in their wing of their castle, sitting by their fire, contemplating their life, and all the many choices, the people, and the wars that were fought so they can wear their crown and sit upon their throne.

We as humans have been spoon-fed codependency. Women have especially been taught that they need a partner to define them. As a woman, I can honestly say that I was not taught to be my full self. I was taught to create a version of me that was appealing to a man who would eventually take me out of my parent's home and into a home of submission, gender roles, and constriction; these equaling a different kind of loneliness.

As queen of myself, I have come to embrace the feelings that surface. After all, I made choices along the way that have enabled me to use these feelings. So, I will stand in my power as queen and reap what I have sown. Not out of rejection or blame, but out of accountability and power!

It takes a true queen to be able to stand alone, look back, and see all the mishaps and own her part in all of them unapologetically. This is a proclamation to the world that as queen, I own my fuck-ups – they helped shape me. I won't repeat them, but I will transmute, shapeshift, and put on my crown – for I have earned it.

# CHAPTER THIRTEEN

# Bonus Deities!

Freya is not the only deity capable of inspiring a sexual liberation. There are a few more that are fun to call upon and quite literally embody. This is my bonus chapter of deities to inspire, activate, liberate, and stimulate your energetic, physical, and spiritual senses to create a more luscious and decadent day-to-day ritual experience. ENJOY!

**Medusa:** Medusa was a priestess who served in the Temple of the Unruly and Unjust. She was raped by the God of the Sea, Poseidon. He lusted after her beauty, and Athena, who was in love with Poseidon, became enraged with jealousy and cursed none other than Medusa – the victim. Athena turned Medusa into a hideous Gorgon, and anyone who dared to look her in the eyes would be turned to stone.

Medusa is now an icon for women and men who have experienced rape or sexual assault. As a tattoo, she represents female strength, empowerment, endurance, and survival. She has become the ultimate cover girl for victims wanting to show some teeth.

As a snake goddess, she is a symbol of rebirth. As women who shed each month, Medusa offers a mirror of not only acceptance of one's reproductive cycles but also empowerment through blood activation. Snakes shed and are reborn, just as women who shed the lining of their uterus – a physical death – are rebuilt and reborn every 28 days.

Medusa is a sexual priestess, as she now, in this modern day, is the survivor! She represents one that is taking back her power, no longer a victim; she turns evil ones into stone and owns her sexual prowess.

Many images of Medusa now show her to be very attractive, curvaceous, and confident. No longer is she depicted as a hideous monster to fear and men to loathe. She is the number-one deity I call to in ritual during the month of October, as she is deeply connected to death and rebirth.

There have been many Samhain gatherings where I have channeled her to slither around the room during rituals and offer guests the opportunity to shed the old and prepare to embrace and create something new and beyond powerful.

Listen to the song *Medusa This Is Me* by Reverstorm, and light a green or gold candle. Think of yourself as one covered with scales and slowly begin to move along with the music, allowing yourself to shed – dropping scales, one at a time. These scales should represent attributes, beliefs, old wounds, or traumas that no longer serve you. Allow these scales to fall onto the ground or into an energetic fire that you are dancing with as one of the flames. Invite and welcome a rebirth through the death.

*"Stories are powerful, Medusa said. That's why the male Olympians shaped the myths to celebrate and protect themselves. Look at those stories carefully. They either transform women into objects that have no voice, like a tree or a spider, or else they turn them into monsters."*

Katherine Marsh, *Goodreads*

**Bastet:** If you want the Egyptian version of Freya, then you need look no further than Bastet. Once revered as a lioness goddess, over time she has shifted into more of a feline housecat?! Bastet is a seductress and devourer of life.

She is a protector of women, a deity of sacred sexuality, and a defender of child-birthing women. Bastet is known to have over 300,000 mummified cats in her temple. She is the ultimate feline ambassador and the reason why it was a crime to harm cats in Egypt.

What I adore is her transformation from lioness to domestic cat. The lioness is a symbol and animal that represents fierce strength and protection. There is a certain aspect of emotional distance with lioness energy, a kind of unapproachable energy. With the softening of her moving from this abstract of the unapproachable to the domestic cat, she becomes a deity that is more within one's grasp, a deity one feels more comfortable connecting with.

The two aspects create a polarity within that everyone can relate to. One could liken it to a shadow self being the lioness – or vice versa. Multifaceted deities are easier to relate to.

Call on Bastet when you need protection for your home, animals, children, or self.

She can come in fierce with the roar of a lioness or rub up against you like the most docile house cat. Whichever aspect you call on, you can be assured that she will bring her sharp claws and teeth and her agility to assist you in your endeavor.

For Bastet, I like to burn turquoise-colored candles on a platter surrounded with carnelian stones.

Years ago, I moved through a house protection spell where I filled a jar with my cat's fur (just pet or brush your cat to remove the fur), amethyst, and carnelian stones. I placed the capped jar behind my front entrance, and I recently found the jar, some 20 years later, as I was packing up to move.

If you want good luck, call to Bastet. If you want to be more confident in your own skin, call to Bastet. Bastet is the black cat of superstitions – only, as witches, we do not believe in superstitions. We know better! A black cat crossing your path may be an aspect of none other than Bastet, reminding you that you are protected by your craft.

It should be noted that Sekhmet and Bastet, like Frigg and Freya, are believed to both be aspects of one deity. Again, formulate your own relationship with both, or one as both – the connection is up to you!

When calling upon any Egyptian deity, having an actual cat nearby will increase your activation connection. Cats are very susceptible to the energies that surround us.

*"In ancient times, cats were worshipped as gods; they have not forgotten this."*

Terry Pratchett

**Venus:** While I tend to personally steer clear of the Greek and Roman deities, other than Medusa, I feel that mentioning Venus for the purpose of this book is pretty self-explanatory. Venus is, after all, the Goddess of Love! She is the Roman version of Bastet and Freya, with Aphrodite being the Greek version.

Venus, the second planet from the sun – known as Earth's twin. In Latin, 'Venus' means 'beauty, charming, and lovely'. The Romans named the planet after their cherished goddess because it was the brightest and most beautiful object in the night sky.

Venus is a goddess frequently called on by lovers. She is said to activate desire, lust, and carnal knowledge of the flesh. She is also called upon by the lonely who are seeking companionship, sex, and devotion.

Years ago, I attended a Goddess Conference at a resort called Venus Rising. The location was in North Carolina, and the property was stunning, surrounded by the Appalachian Mountains. The women in attendance were gathered for one main intention – to activate 'self-love.'

Self-love is a modern-day metaphysical practice, and to some a knee-jerk imbalance covered up by bubble baths, champagne, floral-scented lotions, pink manicured nails, and coconut oil-infused hair. What does it really mean to activate self-love?

While I love me a good bubble bath, my idea of self-love is a dirt-covered guttural cry in the heat of the desert after a series of rebirthing life fuckery! To each their own.

One doesn't need to call upon Venus to activate self-love; one simply needs to love every part of oneself – even the not scented or heavily saturated parts.

Venus, as you can tell, is not a deity that I have personally ever called upon.

However, once again, we see a shadow side and polarity in the question of whether Venus and Aphrodite are one and the same. When you pull in the mythology of Venus, being a battle goddess and one who achieves great victory, and then you look at Aphrodite, who is also Goddess of Love and War...it is pretty safe to say that the Greeks and the Romans had some very clear similarities with both of these deities.

Both Aphrodite and Venus are deeply connected to Ishtar, the Mesopotamian Goddess of Sexuality and War – a deity that I have spent some time with. Ishtar was known as the Queen of Heaven. She too is complex! She possesses conflicting attributes of love, fertility, war, and justice.

> *"Desire is a quest for the beautiful – whatever 'the beautiful' might mean. Desire is the thing that makes us feel great about the world and therefore be great in it. It is the life force that spurs us on to do, to be, to think."*
> Bettany Hughes, from *Venus and Aphrodite: A Biography of Desire*

**Dionysus:** It is only fitting that we invite the one and only Dionysus! God of flowing wine, sex, fertility, revelry, theatre, and madness. One of my favorite gods, and no, it's not just because of his fondness for wine – although that is a bonus!

Dionysus should be considered the icon for the LGBTQIA+ community. Back in 2019, I was actively leading a very large Wiccan/Pagan community, and I wanted to do more open events. I asked my dear friend Kaleb to offer service with me as my acting high priest. We were hosting our annual Mabon event and decided to invoke Dionysus.

Kaleb wore a long, loose, dark blue robe, and I wore a red velvet skintight dress. We both wore gold leaf crowns upon our heads. The altar was covered with freshly baked breads, red and green grapes, dark chocolate-covered pomegranates, and, of course, plenty of red wine. We sat upon our thrones and invited each guest to stand up at the altar and share their moments of abundance that they had harvested during the season. After each guest made their offering, we all took a sip of wine.

It was a decadent event, and afterwards we all gathered around the fire to celebrate as a community. Dionysus is one who just gives zero fucks! He is a god that enjoys the moment, and if he starts to not enjoy the moment, then another sip of wine will surely help.

Dionysus is the male counterpart to my life card in the tarot – the Empress. Both possess a relaxed, slow-down vibe – stay in the moment and celebrate the abundance in your life. As a god of sex, Dionysus encourages the debauchery and play between everyone, anytime, anyplace. He is a very exuberant, bold, and expressive deity.

In this day and age, we really should take sex off the taboo shelf and embrace the fact that we are all animals with very real, raw, and primal instinctual urges. Sex is something that everyone engages in, and yet we still don't want to talk about it?

Dionysus as a god of wine is all about celebrating the fruits of one's labor.

Grapes represent abundance and fertility, and nothing is quite so luscious as a heavy pour of red wine at the end of a long day. Dionysus is also known as the god Bacchus, or the Roaring God of Wine.

To indulge and connect with Dionysus, do just that – pour yourself a large goblet of wine, light every candle you have, scatter rose petals, settle into that steaming bath, and lie back and bask in the abundance of your life. Take inventory!

A good habit to get into is to, at the end of the day, express gratitude for every amazing moment that happened during that day. Don't dwell and focus on the 'could haves,' 'should haves,' or 'did nots.' Focus instead on what you reaped and enjoyed.

> "He who begets something which is alive must dive down into the primeval depths in which the forces of life dwell. And when he rises to the surface, there is a gleam of madness in his eyes because in those depths lives cheek by jowl with life. The primal mystery is itself mad – the matrix of the duality and the unity of disunity."
> Walter Friedrich Otto, from *Dionysus: Myth and Cult*

Madness, revelry, debauchery! A god devoted to the concept of 'eat, drink, and be merry.' A deity that encourages a wild frenzy! We can liken Dionysus to a wildfire, burning so hot, bright, and out of control that one cannot help but seek out the flame.

We all know someone like Dionysus. Deep down, we all envy the way they burn hot, and heavy, and without a care in the world. What we forget is that we can all be that way in our own lives, in our own way. Dionysus doesn't want us to envy him or compare ourselves to him. Remember, to compare is to compete, and to compete is to defeat. I believe Dionysus wants us to savor each second of our glorious, authentic, and fucked-up lives. He wants us to live just like Freya – bold, confident, and without apology.

We all deserve to sit upon our thrones and celebrate the fact that we chose to get out of bed and live in this chaotic world and make the most of it! If every moment is a gift, why are we not celebrating it? If every day is precious, why do we not appreciate them? We are here to live one bold, loud life. So, let's do just that! Let's love ourselves unabashedly!

## A NOTE OF GRATITUDE

Thank you for taking time in your lives to share in my journey with Freya. This past year has taught me so much, and my heart was overflowing with all the lessons, magic moments, high tides, and low that I simply had to share.

Freya was a catalyst. While I initially called on her to be my liberation as a single woman, what she brought me was the most unexpected adventure and ultimate love. My single life was short! I now know that it's true what people say – when you get out of your own way, all things are possible.

It was not my intention to fall in love. My husband and I liken it to the universe slamming us together at a time when we were both not resisting the natural flow and rhythm of life. We met because of universal timing, and we have zero regrets, only gratitude.

Freya helped me to shed the old stereotypical societal roles and redefine. Killing the wife was one of the most painful and powerful nights of my life, and one I will never forget. Moving through the selkie ritual was profound.

Looking back, I am grateful for Freya and the mirrors she showed me, even if at times I didn't like what was being reflected. My big takeaway is presence. To be fully engaged in each moment without expectations has been so liberating.

I wish you all a fabulous, no-fucks life! I hope you find the kind of love that I have finally found. It may have taken me 44 years, but it could have taken longer. I hope you find love so passionate that it takes your breath away. Not a day goes by that I do not look at my husband and thank the gods for such an amazing human being.

This life, though filled with fuckery – moments that rip your heart out, human frustrations, good days, bad days, and all the in-betweens – is truly beautiful chaos. Find your inner Freya – embody her! Rise up and be king and/or queen. Build your castle, find your people, taste love so sweet there won't be any room for the bitter, and live loud!

LADY WOLF.

Lady Wolf is a triple-ordained Wiccan high priestess, representing the lineages of Dianic, Hermetic, and Eclectic. In September 2018, she was ordained and titled 'Lady Wolf' by none other than Zsuzsanna Budapest.

Lady Wolf is a master herbalist, green witch, shapeshifter, mother of the Desert Sage witchcraft tradition, animist witch, tarot oracular, avid gardener, reflexologist, desert brat, mother, grandmother, and, finally, a happy wife!

In September 2025, she married her best friend, soulmate, and sailor, and together they live in Southern Utah with their two Corgi puppies, Rocky and Buster. Lady Wolf is a labyrinth facilitator and creatrix, having built four spiral labyrinths here in the High Desert.

Lady Wolf is passionate about spirit animal work and loves to travel and visit groups, communities, covens, and groves where she assists guests in connecting with their primary spirit animal.

She has written four books anchored into animistic witchcraft and is actively working on her sixth book, *Lilith – Queen of the Damned or Damned to be Queen*.

You can contact Lady Wolf for public speaking engagements via the following:

desertsagewitchcraft@gmail.com

Facebook: @LadyWolf

www.ladywolfauthor.com